Through the year with
WORDS OF WISDOM

Through the year with
WORDS OF WISDOM

Compiled by Daniel P. Cronin

Foreword by
Cardinal Basil Hume, O.S.B.

 St Paul Publications

St Paul Publications
Middlegreen, Slough SL3 6BT, England

Copyright © St Paul Publications 1988
First published in Great Britain November 1988
Reprinted September 1989
Cover design: Mary Lou Winters FSP
Printed by Dotesios Printers Ltd, Trowbridge, Wiltshire
ISBN 085439 284 X

St Paul Publications is an activity of the priests and brothers of
the Society of St Paul who proclaim the Gospel through the media
of social communication

Contents

Foreword

Father Danny Cronin has brought together in this book an interesting collection of thoughts, one for each day. People today often find that they do not have time for reading spiritual books, others are not accustomed to the practice of spiritual reading. This book will help those who want something brief, and it may be an encouragement to others to read books that feed our faith. Some of the quotations are from non-Christians, but these, too, can be helpful, for we recognise that all human wisdom comes from God. God often speaks to us through others, through their understanding of the Scriptures or of the great truths of religion.

There is much in this book to feed the spirit. I recommend it, hoping especially that it will prompt and inspire quiet meditation and fervent prayer.

Basil Hume

Welcome!

Welcome to the world of thoughts and quotations. The inspiration for this collection has come from many readers of *The Universe* newspaper who have written to me over the last two years, asking me to assemble in book form some of the items which have appeared in my column "Words of Wisdom". In fact most of the material in this book has come from my own collection supplemented by the best contributions from my readers.

I have compiled this book in the hope that it may bring inspiration and comfort to many people; most of all to those in special need – the sick and the housebound, those in hospital or prison, those recently bereaved. It will give me immense pleasure if you have been handed this book by a member of the Society of St Vincent de Paul – a society to which I have had the privilege of being a chaplain since the day I was ordained.

But this book is also intended for anyone who is interested in growing in the spiritual life. I wanted to choose things which will touch the heart and not only remain in the head. I believe it was George Bernard Shaw who said, "Words of comfort skillfully administered are the oldest therapy known to man". This is the reason why some subjects like "Death" are treated rather more fully, because I have come to realise from correspondents just how helpful the written word can be at crisis points in people's lives.

Some pieces have been selected simply because they respond to "what oft was thought, but ne'er so well express'd" (Alexander Pope); others for their humour. I have also kept in mind my brother priests and others who have to speak in public who may find in this book a quotation which will act as a springboard in preparing a homily or talk. I would also like to think that friends from other churches and faiths will find something from their own traditions, as well as being helped by the riches of our Catholic heritage.

By definition any selection is limited. I have made no attempt to make this diary of thoughts comprehensive since my publishers have been kind enough to suggest a second book. So if your favourite quotation, prayer or thought is missing in this edition, please send it to me at the address below for consideration in the next.

Finally, there are a number of people whom I must thank. First of all, Rowanne Pasco who during her time as Editor of *The Universe* invited me to initiate the "Words of Wisdom" column. From the outset she and I have shared the vision that a book may one day emerge from this project and I am most grateful to her that it has now seen the light of day. To Susanne Mitchell for much professional advice. To St Paul Publications for their confidence and support in publishing this book. To Mr Tom Murphy, the current editor of *The Universe* for his ready co-operation and backing, and to all the readers who have sent in contributions, whether these have been used or not. But to no one more than the writer of the Foreword, who has encouraged me every inch of the way, with great enthusiasm and much generosity of his time.

I just hope that you derive as much pleasure from reading this collection as I received in compiling it.

If you would like to have your favourite quotation, thought, or prayer considered for the next book these should be sent to:

Fr Daniel Cronin
"Words of Wisdom" Book
Cathedral Clergy House
42 Francis Street
Westminster
London SW1P 1QJ

It would help enormously if you can also include which book you have seen your contribution in, the publisher and author's name.

JANUARY

1

I said to the man who stood at the gate of the Year, "Give me a light that I may tread safely into the unknown." And he replied, "Go out into the darkness and put your hand into the hand of God. That shall be to you better than light and safer than a known way."

Minnie Louise Haskins (1875 - 1957)
quoted by King George VI in his Christmas broadcast
25 December, 1939

2

Abandonment

Unhappily there are too many who consider God a threat, who are afraid to pray, for example, the prayer of abandonment of Charles de Foucauld: "Do with me whatever you want", because they fear that having made this total surrender they will find God jeopardizing their well-being by stripping them of what they hold dear. To think this is to distort completely who God is and what His relations are with men. God is our creator, the one who has given us life in the first place, whose one desire for us is that this life may grow and increase to the full. By freely opening ourselves to the activity of God we are, as it were, letting Him continue His work of creating, of bestowing life, so that we are more completely man in proportion to our receptivity for God.

Peter G. Van Breemen, S.J.

3 Abandonment

Father,
I abandon myself into your hands,
do with me what you will.
Whatever you may do,
I thank you.
I am ready for all.
I accept all.
Let your will be done in me
and all your creatures.
I wish no more than this, O Lord.
Into your hands I commend my soul;
I offer it to you with all the love of my heart,
for I love you, Lord, and so need to give myself,
to surrender myself into your hands, without reserve
and with boundless confidence,
for you are my Father.

Charles de Foucauld (1858 - 1916)

4 Acceptance

Grace strikes us when we are in great pain and restless-
ness. It strikes us when we walk through the dark
valley of a meaningless and empty life. Sometimes at
that moment a wave of light breaks into our darkness,
and it is as though a voice were saying, "You are
accepted. You are accepted, accepted by that which is
greater than you, and the name of which you do not
know. Do not seek for anything, do not perform anything, do not intend anything. Simply accept the fact
that you are accepted."

Paul Tillich (1886 - 1965)

Action

I wondered why somebody didn't do something;
then I realised that I was somebody.

Anon.

Action

If you want to get something done, ask someone who's
already busy.

Common saying

7 Adversity

In prosperity our friends know us; in adversity we
know our friends.

J. Churton Collins (1848 - 1908)

8 Alone

There is something about being alone that is the core of
Christian life. A person cannot truly come to know the
Father by constant activity; rather, real Christian action,
real love for others, springs from hearing the voice of
God in times of rest and quietness. The life of Jesus
himself bears this out, for his power to do good among
men was derived from the time he spent alone, in the
desert or on a mountain, in prayer before God.

Roger Repohl

9 Alone

I live alone; dear Lord, stay by my side.
In all my daily needs be thou my guide.
Grant me good health, for that indeed I pray,
To carry on my work from day to day.
Keep pure my mind, my thoughts, my every deed.
Let me be kind, unselfish, in my neighbour's need.
Spare me from fire, from flood, malicious tongues,
From thieves, from fear and evil ones.
If sickness or an accident befall,
Then humbly, Lord, I pray,
Hear thou my call.
And when I'm feeling low or in despair,
Lift up my heart, and help me in my prayer.
I live alone, dear Lord, yet have no fear
Because I feel your presence very near.

10 Alone

Alone with none but thee, my God,
I journey on my way;
What need I fear, when thou art near,
O King of night and day?
More safe am I within thy hand,
Than if a host did round me stand.
My destined time is fixed by thee,
And death doth know his hour.
Did warriors strong around me throng,
They could not stay his power;

No walls of stone can man defend
When thou thy messenger dost send.

My life I yield to thy decree,
And bow to thy control
In peaceful calm, for from thine arm
No power can wrest my soul.
Could earthly omens e'er appal
A man that heeds the heavenly call?

The child of God can fear no ill,
His chosen dread no foe;
We leave our fate with thee, and wait
Thy bidding when to go.
'Tis not from chance our comfort springs,
Thou art our trust, O king of kings.

Hymn from the Prayer of the Church

11 Asking

I asked God for strength to achieve success;
He made me weak so that I could humbly learn to
obey.
I asked for good health to accomplish great things;
He gave me infirmity so that I could do better things.
I asked for riches so that I could be happy;
He gave me poverty so that I could be wise.
I asked for power so that I could be admired by men;
He gave me weakness so that I could experience the
        need for God.
I asked for a companion so as not to live alone;
I was given a heart so that I can love all my brothers.

I asked for everything that could make my life joyful;
I was given life so that I could rejoice in all things.
I received nothing of what I asked,
but everything that I hoped for.
And in spite of myself, my unspoken prayers were
    answered.
I am in fact the richest among all men.

Psalm - written by patients in a New York hospital

12 Attitudes

The best thing to give your enemy is forgiveness;
to an opponent, tolerance; to a friend, your heart;
to your child, a good example;
to your father, deference;
to your mother, conduct that will make her
    proud of you;
to yourself, respect; to all men, charity.

Arthur James Balfour (1848 - 1930)

13 Calvary

It is very difficult for us to imagine the scene when this
low mound stood outside the wall of the city and three
crosses on it were silhouetted against the sky. It was
the turning-point of history when Christ hung there,
the God who knew the agony of man. It was a garden
then, with flowers trampled underfoot, and death
where life had been. They took a tree, a thing of
beauty, and nailed the Son of God upon it. The Cross is
the sign of what man has done to God. But it is more
than that. It is the sign of what God has done for man.

It is the emblem, not of defeat, but of victory. Man has striven and still strives against God, and the Cross is the worst that man can do. But he cannot conquer love. Love was eternally triumphant on this hilltop, as on all the Calvaries of human life. Love has conquered the last enemy. There is an empty tomb not far away.

Leslie Farmer

14 Challenge

If you give a man more than he can do, he will do it. If you only give him what he can do, he'll do nothing.

Rudyard Kipling (1865 - 1936)

15 Change

If Christianity be a universal religion suited not simply to one locality or period, but to all times and places, it cannot but vary in its relations and dealings towards the world around it, that is, it will develop. In a higher world it is otherwise, but here below to be perfect is to have changed often.

Cardinal John Henry Newman (1801 - 1890)

16 Change

In our relationship with ourselves we should accept the unchangeable and change the unacceptable.

Bernard O'Brien

17 Change

God grant me the serenity
To accept the things I cannot change,
The courage to change the things I can,
And the wisdom to know the difference.

Reinhold Niebuhr (1892 - 1971)

18 Change

I wanted to change the world. But I have found that
the only thing one can be sure of changing is oneself.

Aldous Huxley (1894 - 1963)

19 Children

Children learn what they live

If a child lives with criticism
He learns to condemn.

If he lives with hostility
He learns to fight.
If he lives with ridicule
He learns to be shy.

If he lives with shame
He learns to be guilty.

If he lives with tolerance
He learns confidence.

If he lives with praise
He learns to appreciate.

If he lives with fairness
He learns about justice.

If he lives with security
He learns to have faith.

If he lives with approval
He learns to respect himself.

If he lives with acceptance and friendship
He learns to find love in the world.

20 Christian

A Christian should always remember that the value of his good works is not based on their number and excellence but on the love of God which prompts him to do these things.

St John of the Cross (1542 - 1591)

21 Christian

I like your Christ, but I do not like your Christians, because they are too unlike your Christ.

Mahatma Gandhi (1869 - 1948)

22 Christian

If a man cannot be a Christian where he is, he cannot be a Christian anywhere.

Henry Ward Beecher (1813 - 1887)

23 Christian

The purpose of Christianity is not to avoid difficulty, but to produce a character adequate to meet it when it comes. It does not make life easy; rather it tries to make us great enough for life.

James L. Christensen

24 Christian

If you were arrested for being a Christian... would there be enough evidence to convict you?

Kenneth E. Kirk

25 Christianity

In the home
        it is kindness;
In society
        it is courtesy;
In business
        it is honesty;
In work
        it is fairness;

Towards the weak
  it is help;
Towards the unfortunate
  it is sympathy;
Towards the wicked
  it is resistance;
Towards the strong
  it is trust;
Towards the penitent
  it is forgiveness;
Towards the successful
  it is congratulations;
And toward God
  it is reverence and obedience.

Anon.

26 Church

The Church after all is not a club of saints; it is a hospital for sinners.

George Craig Stewart

27 Church

The Church is the one thing that saves a man from the degrading servitude of being a child of his own time.

Gilbert Keith Chesterton (1874 - 1936)

28 Commitment

"My God, with all my heart above all things I love you, infinite good and our eternal happiness, and for your sake I love my neighbour as myself and forgive offences received. O Lord, may I love you more and more."

With all my heart. I stress, here, the adjective "all". Totalitarianism in politics is an ugly thing. In religion, on the contrary, a totalitarianism on our side towards God is a very good thing. It is written: "You shall love the Lord your God with all your heart, and with all your soul, and with all your might. And these words which I command you this day shall be upon your heart; and you shall teach them diligently to your children, and walk by the way, and when you lie down, and when you rise. And you shall bind them as a sign upon your hand, and they shall be as frontlets between your eyes. And you shall write them on the doorposts of your house and on your gates" (Deut 6:5-9). That "all" repeated and applied insistently is really the banner of Christian maximalism. And it is right: God is too great, he deserves too much from us for us to be able to throw to him, as to a poor Lazarus, a few crumbs of our time and our heart. He is infinite good and will be our eternal happiness; money, pleasure, the fortunes of this world, compared with him, are just fragments of good and fleeting moments of happiness. It would not be wise to give so much of ourselves to these things and little of ourselves to Jesus.

Pope John Paul I (1912 - 1978)
General audience, 27 September 1978

29 Communion

If I send you all the treasures
    That your heart could ever crave,
They would crumble into dust-heaps:
    They can't last beyond the grave.

But I send you something greater:
    Tho' the token may seem small,
My gift will last for ever –
    'Tis the greatest gift of all.

Rev T. Foy

30 Communion

Holy Thursday, the eve of our Saviour's death, the day on which he instituted the adorable Sacrament of the Eucharist.

This was the most lovely day of Our Lord's life. It was the greatest day of his love and tenderness.
Jesus was on the point of perpetuating his presence in our midst. His love on the Cross was boundless, it is true, but there would be an end to his sufferings, and Good Friday was to last only one day.

Holy Thursday would endure till the end of time. Jesus made himself the Sacrament of himself forever.

St Peter Julian Eymard (1811 - 1868)

31 Compassion

The compassion that you see in the kind-hearted is God's compassion: he has given it to them to protect the helpless.

Sri Ramakrishna

FEBRUARY

1 | Compassion

The root of the matter, if we want a stable world, is a very simple and old fashioned thing, a thing so simple that I am almost ashamed to mention it for fear of the derisive smile with which wise cynics will greet my words. The thing I mean is love, Christian love, or compassion. If you feel this, you have a motive for existence, a reason for courage, an imperative necessity for intellectual honesty.

Bertrand Russell (1872 - 1970)

2 | Compassion

Compassion is receiving comfort and understanding from someone close to you when you are in need, being able to lean on a friend who has suffered emotionally in the same way, and perhaps when time has helped a little in the healing process and the bitterness subsided, to be able to help another person in similar circumstances.

3 | Concern

No man has learned to live
until he can rise above the narrow confines
of his individualistic concerns
to the broader concerns of all humanity.

Length without breadth
is like a self-contained tributary
having no outward flow to the ocean.
Stagnant, still, and stale,
it lacks both life and freshness.
In order to live creatively
and meaningfully,
our self-concern must be wedded to other-concern.

Martin Luther King (1929 - 1968)

4 Conferences

A conference is a gathering of important people who singly can do nothing, but together can decide that nothing can be done.

Fred Allen (1894 - 1957)

5 Contemplation

There are fixed times for all things, and it would manifestly be out of order to do at one moment what we ought to do at another. But there is no time in which we ought not to love God and think of Him.

François Malaval

6 Contemplation

He need have no fear of error in believing that God is calling him to contemplation, regardless of what sort of person he is now or has been in the past. It is not what you are nor what you have been that God sees with His all-merciful eyes, but what you desire to be.

The Cloud of Unknowing

7 Contentment

When we cannot find contentment in ourselves it is useless to seek it elsewhere.

François, Duc de la Rochefoucauld (1613 - 1680)

8 Conversion

Conversion is but the first step in the divine life. As long as we live we should more and more be turning from all that is evil, and to all that is good.

Tryon Edwards (1809 - 1894)

9 Conversion

The moment I realised that God existed, I knew I could not do otherwise than to live for Him alone.

Charles de Foucauld (1858 - 1916)

10 Courtesy

Be nice to people on your way up because you'll meet them on your way down.

Wilson Mizner (1876 - 1933)

11 Creed

What a man believes may be ascertained, not so much from his creed, but from the assumptions on which he habitually acts.

George Bernard Shaw (1856 - 1950)

12 Criticism

What you dislike in another, take care to correct in yourself.

Thomas Sprat (1635 - 1713)

13 Cross, the

No pain, no palm; no thorns, no throne;
no gall, no glory; no cross, no crown.

William Penn (1644 - 1718)

14 Cross, the

The cross in my pocket

I carry a cross in my pocket
A simple reminder to me
Of the fact that I am a Christian
No matter where I may be.

This little cross is not magic
Nor is it a good luck charm.
It isn't meant to protect me
From every physical harm.
It's not for identification
For all the world to see.
It's simply an understanding
Between my Saviour and me.

When I put my hand in my pocket
To bring out a coin or key

The cross is there to remind me
Of the price He paid for me.

It reminds me, too, to be thankful
For my blessings each day
And to strive to serve Him better
In all that I do and say.

It's also a daily reminder
Of the peace and comfort I share
With all who know my Master
And give themselves to His care.

So I carry a cross in my pocket
Reminding no one but me
That Jesus Christ is Lord of my life
If only I'll let Him be.

15 Cross, the

You asked for my hands
that you might use them for your purposes.
I gave them for a moment; then withdrew them, for
the work was hard.

You asked for my mouth
to speak out against injustice.
I gave you a whisper that I might not be accused.

You asked for my eyes
to see the pain of poverty.
I closed them, for I did not want to see.

You asked me for my life
that you might work through me.
I gave you a small part that I might not get
"too involved".

Lord, forgive me for calculated efforts to serve you
only when it is convenient for me to do so,
only in those places where it is safe to do so, and
only with those who make it easy to do so.

Father, forgive me, renew me,
send me out as a usable instrument,
that I may take seriously the meaning of your Cross.

Joe Seramane

16 Death and Bereavement

We seem to give them back to thee, O God, who gavest
them to us. Yet as thou didst not lose them in the giving,
so we do not lose them by their return. Not as the world
giveth, givest thou, O Lover of souls. What thou givest,
thou takest not away, for what is thine is ours also if we
are thine. And life is eternal and love is immortal, and
death is only an horizon, and an horizon is nothing, save
the limit of our sight.

Lift us up, strong Son of God, that we may see further;
cleanse our eyes that we may see more clearly; draw us
closer to thyself that we may know ourselves to be
nearer to our loved ones who are with thee.

And while thou dost prepare a place for us, prepare us also for that happy place, that where thou art we may be also for evermore.

Bede Jarrett, O.P. (d. 1934)

17 Death

Death is not the greatest loss in life. The greatest loss in life is what dies inside us while we live.

18 Death

Christ leads me through no darker rooms,
than he went through before;
he that into God's Kingdom comes
must enter by this door.
My knowledge of that life is small
the eye of faith is dim;
but 'tis enough that Christ knows all,
And I shall be with him.

Richard Baxter (1615 - 1691)

19 Death

I turn to you, Almighty God,
in this my time of grief.
I do not beg for comfort
and I do not ask relief.
I only seek the courage and

the strength to bear my sorrow,
that I may still fulfil my place
and carry on tomorrow.
I do not want to drop my cross
or fall beside the way.
Just give me grace to serve you, God,
for still another day.
Let not my body weaken now,
let not my mind go weary,
however much the skies may seem
to be so dark and dreary;
enable me to do your will,
however great my loss,
and as your humble servant, God,
to bear whatever loss.

20 Death

Pray for me, as I will for thee, that we may merrily meet
in heaven.

St Thomas More (1478 - 1535)

21 Death

Perhaps if we could see
        The splendour of the land
        To which our loved are called
                from you and me,
                WE'D UNDERSTAND.

Perhaps if we could hear
     The welcome they receive
     From old familiar voices –
         all so dear –
     WE WOULD NOT GRIEVE.

Perhaps if we could know
     The reason why they went,
     We'd smile – and wipe away
         the tears that flow:
     WE'D WAIT CONTENT.

Carmelite Monastery, Tallow, Waterford

22 | Death

Death is nothing at all,
I have only slipped away into the next room.
I am I and you are you;
Whatever we were to each other that we are still.

Call me by my old familiar name,
speak to me in the easy way which you always used.
Put no difference into your tone;
wear no forced air of solemnity or sorrow.
Laugh as we always laughed
at the little jokes we enjoyed together.
Play, smile, think of me, pray for me.
Let my name be ever the household word it always was.
Let it be spoken without effect,
without the ghost of a shadow on it.
Life means all that it ever meant.

It is the same as it ever was;
there is absolutely unbroken continuity.

What is this death but a negligible accident;
why should I be out of mind because I am out of sight?
I am but waiting for you, for an interval,
somewhere very near,
just around the corner.
All is well.

Canon Henry Scott-Holland (1847 - 1913)

23 Death

Those we hold most dear never truly leave us... they live on in the kindness they showed, the comfort they shared, and the love they brought into our lives.

24 Death

"I'll lend you for a little while a child of mine," God said,
"For you to cherish while he lives and mourn for when
   he's dead.
It may be six or seven years, or only two or three,
But will you, till I call him home, look after him for me?
He'll bring his love to gladden you and, should his stay
   be brief,
You'll have a host of memories as solace for your grief.
I cannot promise he will stay, since all from earth return,
But there are lessons taught below I want this child
   to learn.

I've looked the wide world over in my search for
          teachers true,
And from the throng that crowds life's lane,
          at last I've chosen you.
Now will you give him all your love,
          nor think your labour vain,
And turn against me when I come to take him back
          again?"

*Sent to me by Irene Smith
who derived much comfort from this passage when she lost
her little boy Dominic in 1986 aged only 13 months*

25 Death

*Paul Joseph Hermes, son of John and Annette Hermes of Kansas City,
died at the age of five... During the service John Hermes read the
reflections that follow:*

Words cannot express our thanks to the many friends
who have given us so much comfort during this time of
great grief, sorrow and loss. I think, however, we owe it
to Paul not to dwell entirely on the grief and sorrow. For
neither grief, sorrow nor sadness were Paul's life-style.
Rather, he knew not grief, nor sorrow, nor sadness, nor
suffering, nor sickness, but what he did know, from the
time he was born until he died in my arms Sunday night,
was love. And love he received. And love he gave – in
abundance.

He knew joy, fun, kindness and concern for everyone.
Everyone Paul met was Paul's friend. He knew no age
barrier and for him it was not just a child's world or an
adult's world. Because his friends covered the entire

panorama of life, young and old and all in between, neither station nor status made any difference to Paul. A typical expression came from a man who said, "I had just gotten to know Paul," and he was glad. Paul lived for a party, for a game, for a good time. He was an idealist. He was very sensitive. I believe the only hurt he knew was to see someone sad. And then he would say anything to make them happy. Therefore, I think a worse tragedy than Paul's death would be to measure his life span by a calendar. It's the normal thing to think it's all right to die at 80 but a tragedy to die at 5. When we think this way it makes Paul's life look a waste. Paul's life was not a waste. But instead it reached a beauty and a fullness, and a fruition in five short years than many, if not most, never reach. Paul knew the qualities that this life is all about. Especially, what it should be about – love and concern.

Therefore, it is our hope and prayer, that while you share our sorrow, you will also help in some way to perpetuate not just Paul's memory, but Paul's style. And in that way, Paul Joseph will live forever.

Quoted from the 'National Catholic Reporter'

26 Death

Remember man as you pass by,
As you are now so once was I,
As I am now so you will be
So remember man eternity.

Written on a gravestone in the Pioneers Cemetery, Australia

27 Death

What is Dying?

I am standing on the sea shore. A ship sails and spreads her white sails to the morning breeze and starts for the ocean. She is an object of beauty and I stand watching her till at last she fades on the horizon, and someone at my side says, "She is gone." Gone where? Gone from my sight, that is all; she is just as large in the masts, hull and spars as she was when I saw her, and just as able to bear her load of living freight to its destination.

The diminished size and total loss of sight is in me, not in her; and just at the moment when someone at my side says, "She is gone," there are others who are watching her coming, and other voices take up a glad shout, "There she comes," and that is Dying.

28 Death

I dreamt death came the other night
and heaven's gate swung wide.
With kindly grace an angel came
and ushered me inside;
and there to my astonishment
stood folks I'd known on earth:
some I had judged quite unfit,
or of but little worth.

Indignant words rose to my lips
but never were set free,
for every face showed stunned surprise.
NO-ONE EXPECTED ME.

Len Dean

29 Decisions

Decisions are my whole life. As long as you make more right decisions than wrong ones, you're ahead of the game, but it's better to be wrong sometimes than not to be able to decide.

Calvin Klein

MARCH

1 | Democracy

Democracy is the recurrent suspicion that more than half of the people are right more than half of the time.

E.B. White

2 | Easter

Lift up your heads ye sorrowing ones;
And be ye glad of heart.
For Calvary Day and Easter Day,
Earth's saddest day and gladdest day,
Are just one day apart.

3 | Education

The test of every religious, political or educational system, is the man it forms. If a system injures the intelligence it is bad. If it injures the character it is vicious. If it injures the conscience it is criminal.

Henri Frederic Amiel (1821 - 1881)

4 | Education

Perhaps the most valuable result of all education is the ability to make yourself do the thing you have to do, when it ought to be done whether you like it or not; it is the first lesson that ought to be learned; and however early a man's training begins, it is probably the last lesson that he learns thoroughly.

Thomas Henry Huxley (1825 - 1882)

Education

When you educate a man you educate an individual, when you educate a woman you educate a whole family.

Dr Charles Duncan McIver (1860 - 1906)

Education

New ideas on education come in fairly frequent cycles. If you are five years out of date, you are very far behind. If you're twenty-five years out, you're likely to be in the forefront of a new advance.

Brother Clare

Encouragement

Our chief want in life is somebody who shall make us do what we can.

Ralph Waldo Emerson (1803 - 1882)

Equality

There is no comparison between men and women. It is like trying to compare a rose with a jasmine. Each has its own perfume. Women are not equal to men. But then men are not equal to women.

Islamic poem

9 Evil

All that is necessary for the victory of evil is that good men do nothing.

Edmund Burke (1729 - 1797)

10 Experience

What I had always desired, even when I was quite young, was the gift of experiencing everything with the greatest possible intensity. It is still my quest now: intensity of experience which gives significance to every fleeting moment. In this lies the secret of happiness which must, of needs, include both sorrow and joy, the little sorrows and the little joys, as well as the great sorrows and the great joys. Rejection of experience may shield one from many adversities and disappointments, but at a very heavy price.

Prince Leopold of Loewenstein

11 Faith

Faith that goes on trusting even when there seems to be no reason for trust is, in the most literal sense, God's work and God's gift. God bestows this gift on all who ask for it. He may not do so in just the way we want, or at the time we expect. Being willing to leave the manner

41

and the time of this gift to God the giver is itself part of
faith, a test of our sincerity in asking for faith.

John Jay Hughes

12 Faith

All work that is worth anything is done in faith.

Albert Schweitzer (1875 - 1965)

13 Faith

It is never a question with any of us of faith or no faith;
the question always is, "In what or in whom do we put
our faith?"

Anon.

14 Fanaticism

A fanatic is one who can't change his mind and won't
change the subject.

Sir Winston Churchill (1874 - 1965)

15 Fathers

When I was a boy of fourteen, my father was so ignorant
I could hardly stand to have the old man around. But
when I got to be twenty-one, I was astonished at how
much he had learned in seven years.

Mark Twain (1835 - 1910)

16 Fathers

The child is not likely to find a father in God unless he finds something of God in his father.

Robert Ingersoll (1833 - 1899)

17 Fear

Half the things that people do not succeed in, are through fear of making the attempt.

James Northcote

18 Flattery

He who praises everybody praises nobody.

Dr Samuel Johnson (1709 - 1784)

19 Forgiveness

O Lord, remember not only the men and women of goodwill, but also those of ill-will. But do not remember all the suffering they have inflicted on us, remember the fruits we have bought, thanks to this suffering – our comradeship, our loyalty, our humility, our courage, our generosity, the greatness of heart which has grown out of all this, and when they come to the judgement, let all the fruits that we have borne be their forgiveness.

Found scribbled on a piece of paper near the body of a dead child at Ravensbruck camp where 92,000 women and children died

20 Forgiveness

To err is human, to forgive, divine.

Alexander Pope (1688 - 1744)

21 Forgiveness

God pardons like a mother who kisses the offence into everlasting forgetfulness.

Henry Ward Beecher (1813 - 1887)

22 Forgiveness

I can forget my earlier sins and failings: they rest in the bosom of God's mercy. What is important is that I should put my present life in order.

Cardinal Augustin Bea, S.J. (1881 - 1969)

23 Forgiveness

Jesus appreciates the goodwill that brings us back to Him every time I fail Him by my sins. Though I consider myself unworthy of Him because I return for my own "selfish" reasons, He is glad that I return. Like the father of the prodigal son, He asks no questions and offers no criticism, but rejoices that I have come back to his house for forgiveness, assistance, and the chance to try again.

Anthony J. Paone, S.J.

24 Freedom

There are two freedoms – the false where a man is free to do what he likes; the true, where a man is free to do what he ought.

Charles Kingsley (1819 - 1875)

25 Freedom

Freedom is not worth having if it does not include the freedom to make mistakes.

Mahatma Gandhi (1869 - 1948)

26 Friendship

Oh the comfort – the inexpressible comfort – of feeling safe with a person,
Having neither to weigh thoughts
Nor measure words –
but pour them all right out – just as they are,
Chaff and grain together – certain that a faithful hand
Will take and sift them –
Keep what is worth keeping –
And then, with the breath of kindness,
Blow the rest away.

Dinah Maria Mulock Craik

27 Friendship

A friend is someone who knows all about you, and loves you just the same.

Elbert Hubbard (1856 - 1915)

45

Friendship

Anyone who looks for a friend without faults will be without friends.

Friendship

God, why is it so hard to get close to people. To let people get close to me. To make friends? Is it because I have been hurt before and I am afraid to be vulnerable again? Your Son had twelve close friends. One sold him for thirty pieces of silver. Another denied that he ever knew him. The rest ran away when he needed them most. Jesus even predicted these things. Yet he didn't shut himself off from friendship. Make me willing to take the risk too. Help me to realise that ultimately, in opening to another human being, I am opening myself to you. Amen.

Friendship

Friendship is the nearest thing we know to religion. God is love, and to make religion akin to friendship is simply the highest expression conceivable by man.

John Ruskin (1819 - 1900)

31 Friendship

This my Friend

Let me tell you how I made his acquaintance.
I heard much of him, but took no heed.
He sent daily gifts and presents,
but I never thanked him.
He often seemed to want my friendship,
but I remained cold.
I was homeless, and wretched and starving,
and in peril every hour,
He offered me shelter, and comfort,
and goods and safety, but
I was ungrateful still.
At last he crossed my path, and with tears
in his eyes he besought me, saying:
"Come and abide with me..."

Let me tell you how he treats me now:
He supplies all my wants; he gives me
more than I dare ask;
He anticipates my every need;
He begs me to ask for more.
He never reminds me of my past ingratitude,
He never rebukes me for past follies.
Let me tell you further what I think of him.
He is as good as he is great...
His love is as ardent as it is true...

MARCH

He is as lavish of his promises as he is faithful
in keeping them,
He is as jealous of my love as he is deserving of it.
I am in all things his debtor,
but he bids me call him FRIEND,
JESUS CHRIST.

Robert Hugh Benson (1871 - 1914)

APRIL

1 Friendship

Permit your friends to be themselves. Accept them as they are. Be grateful for what is there, not annoyed by what friends cannot give. Accept each one's imperfections and individuality and don't feel threatened if their opinions and tastes differ from yours.

Give praise and encouragement. Tell your friends what you like about them, how thankful you are for their presence in your life. Delight in their talents, applaud their successes.

2 Friendship

When in doubt, do the friendliest thing.

Poster

3 Friendship

I believe in hands that work, in minds that think, in hearts that love. A friendly look and a smile often say more than friendly speech.

Cardinal Stefan Wyszynski

4 Friendship

There's nothing worth the wear of winning
But laughter and the love of friends.

Hillaire Belloc (1870 - 1953)

Friendship

Friendships begun in this world will be taken up again, never to be broken off.

St Francis de Sales (1567 - 1622)

Generosity

A man can do a great deal in this world if he doesn't mind who takes the credit.

P.P. Parker

7 Gift

What you are
    is God's gift to you,
What you become
    is your gift to God.

8 Gift

A cheerful giver does not count the cost of what he gives. His heart is set on pleasing and cheering the person to whom the gift is given.

Dame Julian of Norwich (1343 - 1443)

9 God

Each of us has a capacity for God and an ability to relate to him in a personal way. When we do, he brings to us

pardon for the past, peace for the present, and a promise
for the future.

Ralph S. Bell

10 God

God would not be God if he could be fully known to us,
and God would not be God if he could not be known at
all.

H.G. Wood

11 God

You can say all kinds of things about God, but nothing
that you can say will really be worthy of him.

St Augustine of Hippo (354 - 430)

12 God

God is more anxious to bestow his blessings on us than
we are to receive them.

Ibid.

13 God

Let nothing disturb thee,
Let nothing afright thee.
All passeth away:
God alone abideth.
Patience obtaineth all things.
He who hath God

Can want for nothing.
God alone sufficeth.

St Teresa of Avila (1512 - 1582)

14 God

A comprehended God is no God.

St John Chrysostom (345 - 407)

15 God

We need only to put everything into the hands of the good God, to be sure that all will go well.

St Julie Billiart (1751 -1816)

16 God

Not that God's willingness to give depends upon our willingness to ask, of course not. But our capacity to receive does depend upon having enough humility, even brokenness of spirit, to be able to ask. And those who do ask for help in coping, do receive. They discover within them a power beyond their own power... When we turn to God for help we allow him to act through the whole of us.

Richard Harries

17 God

Whatever the cause, God has been profoundly real to me in recent months. In the midst of outer dangers I have felt an inner calmness and known resources of strength which only God could give. In many instances I have felt the power of God transforming the fatigue of despair into the buoyancy of hope. I am convinced that the universe is under the control of a loving purpose and that in the struggle for righteousness man has a cosmic companionship. Behind the harsh appearances of the world there is a benign power. To say God is personal is not to make him an object among other objects or attribute to him the finiteness and limitations of human personality; it is to take what is finest and noblest in our consciousness and affirm its perfect existence in him. It is true that human personality is limited, but personality as such involves no necessary limitations. It simply means self-consciousness and self-direction. So in the truest sense of the word, God is a living God. In him there is feeling – responsive to the deepest yearnings of the human heart; this God both evokes and answers prayers.

Martin Luther King (1929 - 1968)

18 God

God's presence is not discerned at the time when it is upon us, but afterwards, when we look back on what is gone and over.

Cardinal John Henry Newman (1801 - 1890)

19 God

Every sunrise is a message from God;
Every sunset his signature.

20 God

"Lord, I have a problem – it's me."
"My dear child, I have the answer – it's ME!"

21 God

I believe that God loves each one of us without condition, no matter what we ever do or say or think or feel. We are free to accept that love, respond to that love, or reject that love and try to go it alone.

Nina Herrmann

22 Goodness

From good men goodness may be learned.

Aristotle (384 - 322 BC)

23 Goodness

Help us never to demand standards from others which we never even attempt to live up to ourselves; never to contradict with our lives that which we say with our lips; never to be one thing to people's faces and another behind their back.

Help us never to make a promise and then break it because it is difficult to keep; never to do anything dishonourable, either to avoid trouble or to make gain; never to be disloyal to a friend or untrue to a loved one.

Help us never to teach or persuade anyone to do a wrong thing; never to give an example which will make it easier for someone else to go wrong; never to laugh at anyone else's beliefs, and never to hide our own.

Help us to live, that we shall never bring disgrace to others, or grief to you.

William Barclay (1907 - 1978)

24 | Good News

Everyone has inside himself
a piece of good news.
The good news is that you really don't know
how great you can be,
how much you can love,
what you can accomplish, and
what your potential is.
How can you top good news like that?

Ann Frank, Diary

25 | Gossip

Gossip is the art of saying nothing in a way that leaves practically nothing unsaid.

Walter Winchell (1879 - 1972)

26 | Grace

Heavenly Father,
We thank you for health and remember the sick.
We thank you for friends and remember the lonely.

We thank you for food and remember the hungry.
May the remembrance of your many gifts
Help us to use them for the betterment of mankind.

Grace of the present moment

Our salvation is the work of every day of every moment
of our lives. There could be no better time that this very
moment, which God in his mercy gives us. It is an opportunity granted us today which, for all we know, may
not be ours tomorrow. Our salvation does not depend
upon resolutions for the future but on our acting now, at
this instant. The uncertainty of life for all of us ought to
teach us the importance of directing all our energies to
this end; from this alone we should learn how unworthy
any other occupation is that does not lead us to God
who is our ultimate goal.

François Fénelon (1651 - 1715)

27 Handicapped, the

Heaven's very special child

A meeting was held quite far from earth.
"It's time again for another birth,"
Said the angels to the Lord above,
"This special child will need much love.

"His progress may seem very slow,
Accomplishments he may not show,
And he'll require extra care
From the folk he meets down there.

"He may not run, or laugh, or play,
His thoughts may seem quite far away
In many ways he won't adapt
And he'll soon be known as handicapped.

"So let's be careful where he's sent,
We want his life to be content.
Please, Lord, find the parents who
Will do a special job for You.

"They will not realize right away
The leading role they're asked to play,
But with this child sent from above
Comes stronger faith and richer love.

"And soon they'll know the privilege given
In catering for this gift from Heaven;
Their precious charge, so meek and mild
Is Heaven's very special child."

28 Handicapped, the

To Simon, my handicapped son

> (Someone once told me that
> Simon was my masterpiece.)

"You are my masterpiece,"
Whispered one lone voice
And, knowing that the word was murmured not
In idleness, merely to comfort,
I pondered its meaning.
Reflected on its truth.

APRIL

"You are my failure,"
The world had said
And, from those early, non-forgotten years
When my grief was new,
That bitter guiltiness of failure
Haunts me still.

"You are my burden,"
They had said,
Some with voice of scorn,
Some with uneasy pity,
And others with dismay.
But each spoke a message void of hope –
That this burden must be cast aside,
Hidden in some nameless place,
Lest you should fill my life
With wasted years.

But you have filled my life
With growing years.

You came to my unwilling
And uncomprehending care
In a closed, eternal night
That had no days.
But, in the tomb of all those dayless years
There stirred new wakenings,
Rousings from small complacencies
And little, shallow dreams
To finding of new values,
Rich and deep.

Slowly there grew profound new wisdoms,
Quiet strengths there came
And such openings of love,
That love became the reason and the growth
Love became the wisdom and the strength
And love now becomes the vision
That can see, indeed,
"The Masterpiece".

So! when my masterpiece
Shall grace the hall of Heaven,
O, then may he plead for me.

Patricia Davis

29 Handicapped, the

The Beatitudes of the Mentally Handicapped

Blessed are you who take time to listen to difficult speech, for you help us to know that if we persevere we can be understood.

Blessed are you who walk with us in public places, and ignore the stares of strangers, for in your companionship we find havens of relaxation.

Blessed are you who never bid us to "hurry up" and more blessed are you, who do not snatch our tasks from our hands to do them for us, for often we need time rather than help.

59

Blessed are you who stand beside us as we enter new and untried ventures, for our failures will be outweighed by the times we surprise ourselves and you.

Blessed are you who ask for our help, for our greatest need is to be needed.

Blessed are you when by all ways you assure us that the things that make us individuals are not our peculiar muscles, nor our wounded nervous systems, nor in our difficulties in learning, but in the God-given self which no infirmities can confine.

Rejoice and be exceedingly glad, and know that you give us reassurances that could never be spoken in words, for you deal with us as Christ dealt with his children.

Anon.

30 Happiness

Those who bring sunshine to the lives of others cannot keep it from themselves.

James M. Barrie (1860 - 1937)

MAY

1 Happiness

If anyone could tell you the shortest, surest way to all happiness and perfection, he must tell you to make it a rule to yourself to thank and praise God for everything that happens to you. For it is certain that whatever seeming calamity happens to you, if you thank and praise God for it, you turn it into a blessing.

William Law (1686 - 1761)

2 Happiness

Grief can take care of itself, but to get the full value from joy you must have somebody to divide it with.

Mark Twain (1835 - 1910)

3 Happiness

Out of the gloom a voice said unto me,
"Smile and be happy: things could be worse."
So I smiled and was happy and, behold,
things did get worse.

4 Holiness

Sanctity and perfection do not so much depend upon doing extraordinary actions, as upon doing our ordinary actions extraordinarily well. We shall do them ex-

61

traordinarily well if we do them with a pure intention, for the love of God; and if we take care to season them with frequent and fervent aspirations to God. Thus, like the ancient saints, shall we work with God and be perfect. This is the surest way to perseverance.

Bishop Richard Challoner
Vicar Apostolic, London District (1758 - 1781)

5 Holiness

Others should find us easy, approachable, warm but they should detect something else. It is a "something else" built up through years of fidelity, striving, having one's treasure elsewhere.

Cardinal Basil Hume, O.S.B.

6 Holiness

In our era the road to holiness necessarily passes through the world of action.

Dag Hammarskjöld (1905 - 1961)

7 Holy Spirit

Make me a point of contact, Lord, whereby the Holy Spirit may enter into those I touch, whether by the word I say, the prayer I pray, or the life I live.

8 Holy Spirit

Every time we say, "I believe in the Holy Spirit," we mean that we believe that there is a living God able and willing to enter human personality and change it.

J.B. Phillips

9 Holy Spirit

Holy Spirit, I thank you for being with me this day, for all the happiness your will has brought, and for all the toil and hardships I have had to accept. Forgive me for the times when I have forgotten you amid the cares of life. Forgive me also if I have not accepted any suffering in the same spirit as Christ my Lord. Help me to rest in peace this night, that I may wake truly refreshed and willing to spend a new day in your service. Guard me this night, as the good shepherd guards his flock. Grant that, in your mercy and love, when I close my eyes on this world for the last time, I may wake in the joy of your presence to a new everlasting day.

Harold Winstone (1917 - 1987)

10 Home

What makes a Christian Home

It is a place of love, consideration and understanding.
It is a place where they pray for the homeless.
It is not a place where Father and Mother are always away at Church meetings.

It is a place of family fun and enjoyment.
It is a place where children are welcome.
It is a place of welcome and hospitality.
It is not just a home for the family.
It is a place where the stranger can feel at home.
It is a place where God is given thanks for all things.
It is a place where the family can bring their friends.
It is a place where parents pray for their family.
It is a place where children can learn to pray.
It is not just a clean respectable house.
IT IS A HOME.
A place where Jesus himself would feel at ease,
A place where Jesus lives
And callers who come with doubts, fears and sorrows
will meet him. They will find faith, hope and love, company and understanding.

From the Methodist Diary

11 Hope

I hope that I will always be for each man
what he needs me to be.
I hope that each man's death will diminish me,
but fear of my own
will never diminish my joy of life.
I hope that my love for those whom I like
will never lessen my love
for those whom I do not.
I hope that another man's love for me
will never be a measure of my love for him.

I hope that every man will accept me as I am,
but that I never will.

I hope that I will always ask for forgiveness from others,
but will never need to be asked for my own.
I hope that I will always recognise my limitations,
but that I will construct none.
I hope that loving will always be my goal,
but that love will never be my idol.
I hope that every man will have hope.

College student quoted by Henri J. Nouen

12 Hope

Hope is not the closing of your eyes to the
        difficulty, the risk, or the failure.
It is a trust that
        if I fail now, I shall not fail forever;
and if I am hurt,
        I shall be healed.
It is a trust that
        life is good,
        and love is powerful.

Anon.

13 Humanity

Man is too noble to serve anyone but God.

Cardinal Stefan Wyszynski

14 Humanity

Seek not every quality in one person.

Confucius

15 Humanity

No man is an island, entire of itself;
every man is a piece of the continent, a part of the main,
and therefore never send to know for whom the bell
tolls; it tolls for thee.

John Donne (1571? - 1631)

16 Humanity

God did not make the first human because He needed
company, but because He wanted someone to whom
He could show His generosity and love. God did not tell
us to follow Him because He needed our help, but
because He knew that serving Him would make us
whole.

St Irenaeus (c.130 - c.200)

17 Humanity

When through one man a little more love and goodness, a little more light and truth, comes into the world,
then that man's life has had meaning.

Fr Alfred Delp (executed by the Nazis in 1945)

18 Humanity

Tell me what you are busy about and I will tell you what
you are.

Goethe (1749 - 1832)

19 Humanity

People may differ in tradition, language and religion, but they all have one common denominator: a desire to be treated like human beings.

Stanley C. Allyn

20 Humanity

How is it that our memory is good enough to retain the least triviality that happens to us, and yet not good enough to recollect how often we have told it to the same person?

François, Duc de la Rochefoucauld (1613 - 1680)

21 Humanity

There is so much good in the worst of us
And so much bad in the best of us
That it ill behoves any of us
To find fault with the rest of us.

Attributed to Edward Wallis Hoch (1849 - 1925)

22 Humanity

The salvation of mankind lies only in making everything the concern of all.

Alexander I. Solzhenitsyn, Nobel Lecture, 1970

23 Human relationships

Perhaps few among you have so many dealings with men of different races, different religions, different beliefs and different cultures as I – unworthily – have. In all these dealings I have always found that a great love, a wide-open heart, always opens the hearts of others. This great love must be not mere diplomacy but the result of an inner conviction that we are all children of one God, who has created mankind, who has created each one of us, and whose children we all are.

Cardinal Augustin Bea, S.J. (1881 - 1969)

24 Humility

By commencing humbly, one can reach great things, as Jesus Christ did: from the humiliation of the crib to the glory of the Transfiguration on Mount Tabor.

Frederic Ozanam (1813 - 1853)

25 Immortality

If individuals live only seventy years, then a state, or a nation, or a civilisation, which may last for a thousand years, is more important than an individual. But if Christianity is true, then the individual is not only more important but incomparably more important, for he is everlasting and the life of a state or a civilization, compared with his, is only a moment.

C.S. Lewis (1898 - 1963)

Importance

Jesus Christ never met an unimportant person. That is why God sent his Son to die for us. If someone dies for you, you must be important.

M.C. Cleveland

Importance

We have missed the full impact of the Gospel if we have not discovered what it is to be ourselves, loved by God, irreplaceable in his sight, unique among our fellowmen.

Bruce Larson

Incarnation

He became what we are that he might make us what he is.

St Athanasius of Alexandria (c.296 - 373)

Incarnation

He gave us a vision of God where others could only *speak* of it.

Indifference

Indifference makes accomplices of us all, and we are responsible for other people's actions in a precise ratio to our power to prevent them happening. Every generation, therefore, has events with which it must come to terms, if it hopes to walk a straight path afterwards.

Robert David McDonald

| 31 | Indifference |

There's too much apathy in the world –
But then who cares?

Graffito

JUNE

1 Individuality

I am only one, but I am one. I can't do everything, but I can do something. And what I can do, that I ought to do. And what I ought to do, by the grace of God I will do.

Edward Everett Hale (1822 - 1909)

2 Individuality

If a man does not keep pace with his companions, perhaps it is because he hears a different drumming. Let him step to the music which he hears however different and far away.

Henry David Thoreau (1817 - 1862)

3 Individuality

Learn to limit yourself, to content yourself, with some definite thing, and some definite work; dare to be what you are, and learn to resign with a good grace all that you are not, and to believe in your own individuality.

Henri Frederick Amiel (1821 - 1881)

4 Injustice

Injustice anywhere is a threat to justice everywhere.

Martin Luther King (1929 - 1968)

JUNE

5 Intercession

We can often help others best by not going immediately and directly to them, but by going first to God for them. With his infinite compassion and love added to ours, open to any inspiration that he may give us, as well as being sensitive to their feelings and deeper needs, we can help them better, even if it is difficult to say a comforting word or do a helpful thing.

Anon.

6 Intercession

Into thy hands, O Lord and Father, we commend our souls and our bodies, our parents and our homes, friends and servants, neighbours and kindred, our benefactors and brethren departed, all thy people faithfully believing, and all who need thy pity and protection. Enlighten us with thy holy grace, and suffer us never more to be separated from thee, who art one God in Trinity, God everlasting.

St Edmund of Abingdon (1175 - 1240)

7 Jesus Christ

The Living Christ

Not merely in the words you say, not only
      in the deeds confessed,
But in the most unconscious way is Christ expressed.
Is it the very saintly smile? A holy light
      upon your brow?

Oh no! I felt his presence while you
    laughed just now.
For me, 'twas not the truth you taught, to you
    so clear, to me so dim;
But when you come, you straightaway brought
    a sense of him.
So from your life he beckons me, and from
    your heart his love is shed.
Till I lose sight of you, and see the
    Christ instead.

8 Jesus Christ

If Jesus Christ is not true God, how could he *help* us?
If he is not true man, how could he help *us?*

Dietrich Bonhoeffer (1906 - 1945)

9 Jesus Christ

All my theology is reduced to this narrow compass –
Christ Jesus came into the world to save sinners.

Archibald Alexander (1772 - 1851)

10 Jesus Christ

Consider Jesus of Nazareth, the most generous-hearted
person who ever lived. He never refused a request for
help. Great multitudes followed him, and he healed
them all. He went out of his way to cross racial and
religious barriers. He compassed the whole world in his
love.

Jesus Christ alone stands at the absolute centre of humanity, the one completed, harmonious man. He is the absolute and perfect truth, the highest that humanity can reach; at once its perfect image and supreme Lord.

Charles W. French

11 | Jesus Christ

I am the Light and you do not see me
I am the Way and you do not follow me
I am the Truth and you do not believe me
I am the Life and you do not search for me
I am the Master and you do not listen to me
I am the Chief and you do not obey me
I am your God and you do not pray to me
I am your greatest Friend and you do not love me
If you are not happy do not blame me.

St Francis of Assisi

12 | Jesus Christ

Lord Jesus Christ, the things that hold us back from you are so varied: all those sterile worries, futile pleasures and vain preoccupations. So many things tend to distract or frighten us and make us hold back; pride which makes us too cowardly to accept help from others – timidity which draws us back to self-destruction – remorse for past sins, which flees before the purity of what is holy, as sickness flees from the doctor's remedy. And yet in spite of all, you are stronger than all. Draw us to you ever more strongly. Amen.

Sören Kierkegaard

74

13 Jesus Christ

We become what our conception of Jesus Christ is... In the degree of the truth of our conception of him, our minds grow broader, deeper and warmer; our hearts grow wiser and kinder; our humour deeper and more tender; we become more aware of the wonder of life; our senses become more sensitive; our sympathies stronger; our capacity for giving and for receiving greater; our minds are more radiant with a burning light, and the light is the life of Christ.

Caryll Houselander (1901 - 1954)

14 Jesus Christ

Only to be what he wants me to be
Every moment of every day
Yielded completely to Jesus alone
Every step of the pilgrim way.
Just to be clay in the potter's hands
Only to do what his word commands
Only to be what he wants me to be
Every moment of every day.

15 Jesus Christ

Jesus Christ teaches men that there is something in them which lifts them above this life with its hurries, its pleasures and fears. He who understands Christ's teaching feels like a bird that did not know it has wings and now suddenly realises that it can fly, can be free and no longer needs to fear.

Leo Tolstoy (1828 - 1910)

16 Jesus Christ

I read in a book
that a man called
Christ
went about doing good.
It is very disconcerting
that I am so easily
satisfied with
just going about.

Kagawa of Japan

17 Jesus Christ

The highest and most satisfactory expression which the New Testament reaches for the true understanding of Jesus is to call him the Word of God: he is God's means of communication with the world, God's rational address to mankind.

Alan Richardson

18 Jesus Christ

I see his blood upon the rose
And in the stars the glory of his eyes.
His body gleams amid eternal snows,
His tears fall from the skies.
I see his face in every flower,

The thunder and the singing of the birds
Are but his voice and carven by his power.
Rocks are his written words.
All pathways by his feet are worn,
His strong heart stills the overbeating sea,
His crown of thorns is twined with every thorn,
His cross is every tree.

Joseph Plunkett (1887 - 1916)

19 Jesus Christ

When nations and individuals are in deep trouble

Philosophy says: Think your way out
Indulgence says: Drink your way out
Politics says: Spend your way out
Science says: Invent your way out
Industry says: Work your way out
Communism says: Strike your way out
Fascism says: Bluff your way out
Militarism says: Fight your way out
The Bible says: Pray your way out
Jesus Christ says: I AM THE WAY (out).

20 Jesus Christ

Thank you, Lord Jesus Christ,
for all the benefits which you have given me,
for all the pains and insults you have borne for me.
O most merciful redeemer, friend and brother,
may I know you more clearly,

love you more dearly,
and follow you more nearly,
day by day.

St Richard of Chichester (1198 - 1253)

21 Jesus Christ

What exactly was Jesus like to meet? If one had been a
fellow-guest when he asked himself to dinner with
Zacchaeus, or when he was eating with the Pharisee,
what sort of a man would one in fact have seen and
spoken to? What was his conversation like? Having
asked this question, I looked at the Gospel again, and
quite suddenly a new portrait seemed to stare at me out
of the pages. I had never previously thought of a laughing, joking Jesus, physically strong and active, fond of
good company and a glass of wine, telling funny sto-
ries, using, as every good teacher does, paradox and
exaggeration as among the most effective aids to in-
struction, applying nicknames to his friends, and hold-
ing his companions spellbound with his talk... the first
thing we must learn about him is that we should have
been absolutely entranced by his company. Jesus was
irresistibly attractive as a man. The man whom they
crucified was intensely fond of life, and intensely vital
and vivacious... the twentieth century needs to recap-
ture the vision of this glorious and happy man whose
mere presence filled his companions with delight...
When I am asked about the utility of Christianity I must
point to the consolations of living your life in the companionship of this person who commands your love

and adoration precisely because having been through it all and sympathizing with it all he cheers you up and will not have you sad. Your shame at your own misdoings, and shortcomings, your sense of awe and fear of the divine majesty, your broken heart in the presence of sickness and bereavement melt in the presence of this person into the sheer wonder and delight which the happiness of his presence excites... the magical personality of the most lovable young man that was ever born of woman and walked the earth.

Lord Hailsham of St Marylebone

22 Joy

This is the secret of joy. We shall no longer strive for our own way; but commit ourselves, easily and simply, to God's way, acquiesce in his will and in so doing find our peace.

Evelyn Underhill (1875 - 1941)

23 Kindness

Kindness in words creates confidence,
kindness in thinking creates profundity, and
kindness in giving creates love.

Lao Tzu (c.604 - 531 BC)

24 Kindness

I expect to pass through life but once. If, therefore, there be any kindness I can show, or any good things I can do to my fellow being, let me do it now, and not defer or neglect it, as I shall not pass this way again.

William Penn (1644 - 1718)

 ## Knowledge

It is the province of knowledge to speak, and it is the privilege of wisdom to listen.

Dr Oliver Wendell Holmes (1809 - 1894)

Leadership

Leadership is achieved by ability, alertness, experience; by willingness to accept responsibility; by a knack for getting along with people; by an open mind and a head that stays clear under stress.

E.F. Girard

Leadership

A good leader takes a little more than his share of the blame; a little less than his share of the credit.

Arnold H. Glassgow

 ## Learning

Learn everything that you possibly can, and you will discover later that none of it was superfluous.

Hugh of St Victor (d.1142)

29 Learning

Let us look at our own shortcomings and leave other people's alone; for those who live carefully ordered lives are apt to be shocked at everything, and we might well learn very important lessons from the persons who shock us.

St Teresa of Avila (1515 - 1582)

30 Life

I want to be thoroughly used up when I die, for the harder I work the more I live. Life is no brief candle for me. It is a sort of splendid torch which I have got hold of for the moment and I want to make it burn as brightly as possible before handing it on to future generations.

George Bernard Shaw (1856 - 1950)

JULY

1 | Life

What a horrid thing fear is – it keeps us apart from life instead of participating in it and causes us to waste so much of our God-given time on earth. To "have a go" is the important thing, isn't it – not whether or not we succeed... When I sum up everything my short life has taught me... one thing I'm sure of, if we do faithfully the tasks which come to our hand from day to day, without thinking them either too big or too small, and if we take what life sends, without inquests, or too many "Why me's?"... we may one day earn the privilege of being called a servant of the Lord and enter into the joys of true service.

Sylvia Pedder (when she knew she was dying of cancer)

2 | Life

The glory of God is man fully alive.

St Irenaeus (c.130 - c.200)

3 | Life

Fear not that your life will come to an end, but rather that it shall never have a beginning.

Cardinal John Henry Newman (1801 - 1890)

4 Life

He who provides for this life, but takes no care for eternity, is wise for the moment, but a fool forever.

John Tillotson (1630 - 1694)

5 Life

Love life,
Be grateful for it always
And show your gratitude by not
Shying away from its challenges.
Always try to live a bit
beyond your capacities –
And you'll find your capacities
are greater than you ever dreamed.

6 Life

Live each day as if it were your last,
and one day you will be right.

7 Life

Look to this day,
For it is life,
The very life of life.
In its brief course lies all
The realities and verities of existence,

The bliss of growth, the splendour
of action, the glory of power.

For yesterday is but a dream,
And tomorrow is only a vision.
But today, well lived,
Makes every yesterday a dream of happiness
And every tomorrow a vision of hope.

Look well, therefore, to this day.

Sanskrit proverb

8 Life

The Crabbit Old Woman

What do you see, nurse, what do you see?
Are you thinking when you are looking at me –
A crabbit old woman, not very wise,
Who dribbles her food, makes no reply
When you say in a loud voice, "I do wish you'd try."
Who seems not to notice the things that you do
And forever is losing a stocking or shoe.
Who unresisting lets you do as you will
With bathing and feeding the long day to fill.
Is that what you're thinking, is that what you see?
Then open your eyes, nurse, you're not looking at me!
I'll tell you who I am as I sit here so still.
I'm a small child of ten with a father and mother,
Brothers and sisters who love one another.
A young girl of sixteen with wings on her feet
Dreaming that soon now a lover she'll meet.
A bride at twenty – my heart gives a leap

Remembering the vows that I promised to keep.
At twenty-five I have young of my own
Who need me to build a secure, happy home.
A woman of thirty, my young ones grow fast
Bound to each other with ties that last.
At forty, my young sons have grown and gone
But my man's beside me to see I don't mourn.
At fifty once more babies round my knee
Again we know children, my loved one and me.
Dark days are upon me, my husband is dead.
I look at the future – I shudder with dread.
For my young are all rearing young of their own
And I think of the years and the love I have known.
I'm an old woman now and nature is cruel,
'Tis her jest to make old age look a fool.
The body it crumbles. Grace and vigour depart.
There is a stone where I once had a heart.
But inside this old carcass a young girl still dwells.
And now and again my battered heart swells.
I remember the joys. I remember the pain.
And I'm loving and living life over again.
I think of the years all too few – gone too fast,
And accept the stark fact that nothing can last.
So open your eyes, nurse, open and see
Not a crabbit old woman... look closer,
                    See ME.

9 │ Life

The Nurse's reply

What do we see, you ask, what do we see?
Yes: we are thinking when looking at thee:

We may seem to be hard when we hurry and fuss,
But there's so many of you, and too few of us.
We would like far more time to sit by you and talk,
To bath you and feed you and help you to walk,
To hear of your lives and the things you have done –
Your childhood, your husband, your daughter,
     your son.
But time is against us, there's too much to do –
Patients too many, and nurses too few.
We grieve when we see you so sad and alone
With nobody near you, no friends of your own.
We feel all your pain, and know of your fear
That nobody cares now your end is so near.
But nurses are people with feelings as well,
And when we're together you'll often hear tell
Of the dearest old Gran in the very end bed
And the lovely old Dad, and the things that he said.
We speak with compassion and love, and feel sad
When we think of your lives and the joy you've had.
You leave us behind with an ache in our heart.
When you sleep the long sleep, no more worry or care,
So please understand if we hurry and fuss –
There are so many of you and too few of us.

10 | Listening

The essential thing is to be open to the world of compassion. The wounded man needs, above all, someone
who will listen to him, because in all suffering we seek
first a friend who welcomes us, who appreciates us,
who finds what we have to say important.

It is when you listen to people that you recognise them as having the right to speak, the right to express themselves. If you cut them off, you are telling them that they are not interesting, not worth listening to. And it is that which is fundamentally harmful to the wounded person.

Jean Vanier

11 Listening

God entrusts to all of us one or several persons. To a greater or lesser degree, all received a share of a pastoral gift, the capacity to listen to what hurts other people within themselves. Listen not in order to give advice or to respond with categorical "You must's." Listen to clear the ground and to prepare the way for Christ. Listen to what lies "beneath" the other's heart, until he or she feels hope welling up: it is there, even beneath the heart of someone who is rigid or shattering... Knowing how to listen brings with it even a mystical vision of the human being – that human being capable of experiencing both frailty and radiance, fulfilment and the abyss...

Brother Roger of Taizé

12 Listening

If we learn to listen to God, we can learn to listen to each other. Our selfish-self needs training and practice in the art of listening.

The Christian is to be a ready listener, a humble but generous co-operator, and a warm person who can lighten the darkness and relieve fear, not by himself alone, but by relying on the power of God. The Christian is not there always to "jolly people along", but rather to weep sometimes, be silent sometimes, and rejoice sometimes.

Michael Hollings

13 | Loneliness

A man must get away
now and then
to experience loneliness.
Only those who learn how to live
in loneliness
can come to know themselves
and life.

I go out there and walk
and look at the trees and sky.
I listen to the sounds of loneliness.
I sit on a rock or stump
and say to myself,
"Who are you, Sandburg?
Where have you been,
and where are you going?"

Carl Sandburg (1878 - 1967)

14 | Loneliness

Language has created the word loneliness to express the pain of being alone, and the word solitude to express the glory of being alone.

Paul Tillich (1886 - 1965)

15 Loneliness

Never forget that you are not alone. The Divine is with you, helping and guiding. He is the companion who never fails, the friend whose love comforts and strengthens. Have faith and He will do everything for you.

Aruobindo (Hindu)

16 Love

People today are hungry for love, for understanding love, which is much greater and which is the only answer to loneliness and great poverty. That is why we are able to go to countries like England and America and Australia where there is no hunger for bread. But, there, people are suffering from terrible loneliness, terrible despair, terrible hatred, feeling unwanted, feeling helpless, feeling hopeless. They have forgotten how to smile, they have forgotten the beauty of the human touch. They are forgetting what is human love. They need someone who will understand and respect them.

Mother Teresa of Calcutta

17 Love

To love is to be vulnerable. Love anything, and your heart may be broken. If you will not risk that, then give your heart to no one. Wrap it carefully with hobbies, pets and little luxuries; lock it safe in the coffin of your selfishness. But there – safe, dark, motionless, airless – it will change. It will become unbreakable, impenetrable, irredeemable.

18 Love

I feel that God would sooner we did wrong in loving than never love for fear we should do wrong.

Fr Andrew

19 Love

Stop trying to love God and let God love you.

Fr Eric Doyle, O.F.M.

20 Love

Those who really get involved in knowing the poor realise they are our brothers and sisters. It does not matter what colour, or nationality; it does not matter what religion – it is a great strength in their own lives and in the lives of others. I think this will overcome all hatred. We are trying to make bombs of love, of prayer, of sacrifice, to overcome the world by love, and so bring God's love and the proof that God loves the world as a living reality into the hearts of all.

Mother Teresa of Calcutta, in an interview

21 Love

It is always spring-time in the heart that loves God.

St John Vianney (1786 - 1859)

22 Love

Your love for God is no greater than your love for the least important person you know.

Anon.

23 Love

I am what I am because God chose to make me such. In proportion as I understand my God-given value, and appreciate the importance of my personal gifts and daily activities, I shall find satisfaction and joy in offering every hour of my day to him. Whatever my limitations, no matter how small my daily occupations may seem, God will judge my worth by the amount of love I express through my attitude, disposition and daily conduct. Be my heart large or small, if I fill it with love for him, I shall be giving him as much as is possible to my nature.

Anthony J. Paone, S.J.

24 Love

We cannot help conforming ourselves to what we love.

St Francis de Sales (1567 - 1622)

25 Love

As for that which is beyond your strength, be absolutely certain that Our Lord loves you, devotedly and individually: loves you just as you are. How often that conviction is lacking even in those souls who are most devoted to God! They make repeated efforts to love him, they experience the joy of loving, and yet how little they know, how little they realise, that God loves them incomparably more than they will ever know how to love him. Think only of this and say to yourself, "I am loved by God more than I can either conceive or understand." Let this fill all your soul and all your prayers and never leave you. You will soon see that this is the way to find God... Give yourself up with joy to a loving confidence in God and have courage to believe firmly that God's action towards you is a masterpiece of partiality and love. Rest tranquilly in this abiding conviction.

And St John, who knew all the depth and tenderness of God's love, was constantly ravished by the thought, "He loved us first!" (1 John 4:7-10)

Abbé de Tourville

26 Love

God loved us before we loved, or could love, him. God's love for us rendered possible and actual our love of God. Hence the most fundamental need, duty, honour and happiness of man, is not petition or even contrition, nor again even thanksgiving – these three kinds of prayer which, indeed, must never disappear out of our spiritual lives – but adoration.

Friedrich von Hügel (1852 - 1926)

93

27 Love

God is in love with each human individual, personally and particularly. Each of us can rightly regard the whole of Our Lord's heart and interest as centred on our own self, for Our Lord would have undergone all his passion for any one of us, and each of us was present to his mind just as clearly and as significantly as if there were no one else to redeem. The heart of Our Lord is the heart of a man who is God, and who has all God's infinity of knowledge and power and love. And yet it is a human heart with all the human heart's longing to love and to be loved; and no lover has ever been treated and slighted as bitterly as has "This Tremendous Lover".

Eugene Boylan, O.C.S.O.

28 Love

"You are attempting the impossible," my guide said. "You are trying to be patient and forgiving others, and you have never learned to forgive yourself. You are a fine specimen. You believe that your sins are forgiven and yet you are not at peace. And it shows. It always shows through in the end.

"The commandment, "You must love your neighbour as yourself," works both ways because you must love yourself as you love others. In fact if you don't love yourself you will never be able to love your neighbour properly. We cannot communicate the Good News properly to others unless it has already made us feel good about ourselves.

"Be at peace in your soul and all around you hundreds will be converted."

St Seraphim of Sarov (1759 - 1833)

29 Mary

The perfection accorded to Mary must not produce in us the impression that her life on earth was a kind of heavenly life, very different from ours. In reality, Mary had a life like ours. She knew the daily difficulties and trials of human life; she lived in the darkness that faith involves. No less than Jesus, she experienced the temptation and the suffering of inner struggles. We can imagine how stricken she was by the drama of her Son's Passion. It would be a mistake to think that the life of her who was full of grace was an easy and comfortable life. Mary shared everything that pertains to our earthly condition, with all that is demanding and painful.

We must above all note that Mary was created immaculate in order to be better able to act on our behalf. The fullness of grace allowed her to fulfil perfectly her mission of collaboration with the work of salvation: it gave the maximum value to her cooperation in the sacrifice. When Mary presented to the Father her Son nailed to the cross, her painful offering was entirely pure.

And now the Immaculate Virgin, still in virtue of the purity of her heart, helps us to strive for the perfection realised in her. It is for sinners, that is, for all of us, that she received an exceptional grace. In her role as mother, she strives to make all her earthly children sharers in some way in the favour with which she was personally enriched.

Mary intercedes with her Son to obtain mercy and forgiveness for us. She invisibly stoops to all who are in spiritual anguish in order to comfort them and lead them to reconciliation. The unique privilege of her Immaculate Conception puts her at the service of everyone and constitutes a joy for all who call her Mother.

Pope John Paul II

30 Mary

The Blessed Virgin, by becoming the Mother of God, received a kind of infinite dignity because God is infinite; this dignity therefore is such a reality that a better is not possible, just as nothing can be better than God.

St Thomas Aquinas (c.1225 - 1274)

31 Mary

The whole question of the Virgin birth of Jesus need not afflict the average man. If Jesus is unique, unlike any other person, it is not illogical to believe that his birth was unique.

William Lyon Phelps (1865 - 1943)

AUGUST

1 Mary

There is no more excellent way to obtain graces from God than to seek them through Mary, because her Divine Son cannot refuse her anything.

St Philip Neri (1515 - 1595)

2 Mary

If you are in danger, she will hasten to free you; if you are troubled, she will console you. If you are sick, she will bring you relief. If you are in need, she will help you. She does not look to see what kind of person you have been. She simply comes to a heart that wants to love her.

St Gabriel Possenti (1836 - 1862)

3 Mary

He who is devout to the Virgin Mother will certainly never be lost.

St Ignatius of Antioch (d. c. 110)

4 Martyrdom

It is not the pain but the purpose that makes the martyr.

St Augustine of Hippo (354 - 430)

AUGUST

 ## Martyrdom

The tyrant dies and his rule is over; the martyr dies and his rule begins.

Sören Kierkegaard (1813 - 1855)

 ## Maturity

Maturity is the art of living in peace with that which we cannot change.

7 Mercy

If I ever stand trial, I would wish for a human judge, not a righteous one. Good men are convictors. I would prefer one who has been touched by, humbled by, softened by the awareness of failing. In such, mercy has a foothold.

G.K. Chesterton (1874 - 1936)

8 Mercy

Trust the past to the mercy of God,
The present to his love,
The future to his providence.

St Augustine of Hippo (354 - 430)

 ## Mercy

Love bade me welcome; yet my soul drew back,
    Guilty of dust and sin.

But quick-eyed Love, observing me grow slack
      From my first entrance in,
Drew nearer to me, sweetly questioning,
      If I lacked anything.
"A guest", I answered, "worthy to be here."
      Love said, "You shall be he."
"I, the unkind, ungrateful? Ah, my dear,
      I cannot look on thee."
Love took my hand, and smiling did reply,
      "Who made the eyes but I?"
"Truth, Lord, but I have marred them; let my shame
      Go where it doth deserve."
"And know you not", says Love, "who bore the blame?"
      "My dear, then I will serve."
"You must sit down", says Love, "and taste my meat."
      So I did sit and eat.

George Herbert (1593 - 1633)

10 Merit

The silence that accepts merit as the most natural thing
in the world is the highest applause.

Ralph Waldo Emerson (1803 - 1882)

11 Mothers

O God of grace and love, in thankfulness for all that you
have given us through the loving care and hard work of
our own mothers, we pray for your richest blessing
upon all mothers:

for those with difficult homes, whose children are more
of a problem than a blessing;

for those with loved ones far away and those who are lonely;

for those who find it hard to make ends meet, or go short themselves for the sake of their families;

for those who are nearly at the end of their tether;

for those mothers who are trying to make Christ real to their families;

for those who do not know him as their Saviour, nor how to cast their care on him;

for each one according to her need, hear our prayer, and draw all mothers closer to you today, through your Son Jesus Christ our Lord.

Christopher Idle

12 Mothers

His mother's monument

A priest, one evening, made his weary way
Into a graveyard where his mother lay,
And scarcely had he reached the humble mound,
Than tears stole out to bless the hallowed ground.
Beside the humble grave the priest then knelt
To tell the sorrow that his heart then felt.
Full many a messenger of sorrow went,
To make excuse that yet no monument
Stood guardian o'er his mother's sacred head,
To honour her who lay among the dead.
And then a voice came sweetly from the tomb,

"My monument was builded in my womb,
My greatest laurels, greatest praise were won,
The hour that thou became my priestly son.
Behold the mothers that beside me lie,
Whose monuments point proudly to the sky,
Of all these honoured mothers every one,
Would change her tombstone for a priestly son.
Go then my son, and never more lament
That o'er my grave there stands no monument.
Return thou to the desert sands of sin
And win the lost souls, in heaven whom thou has sent,
Fore'er proclaim thee as my monument."

13 Motives

When a man hasn't a good reason for doing a thing, he
has a good reason for letting it alone.

Sir Walter Scott (1771 - 1832)

14 Neighbours

Love your neighbour, yet pull not down your hedge.

George Herbert (1593 - 1633)

15 Nothing people

They do not lie;
they just neglect to tell the truth.
They do not take;
they simply cannot bring themselves to give.

They do not steal;
they scavenge.
They will not rock the boat;
but did you ever see them pull an oar?
They will not pull you down;
they'll simply let you pull them up
and let that put you down.
They do not hurt you;
they merely will not help you.
They do not hate you;
they merely cannot love you.
They will not burn you;
they'll only fiddle while you burn.
They are nothing people:
the sins-of-omission folk;
the neither-good-nor-bad
and-therefore-worse.

Because the good at least keep busy trying and the bad try just as hard; both have that character that comes from caring, action and conviction.

So give me every time an honest sinner, or even a saint. But God and Satan get together, and protect me from the nothing people. Amen.

Anon.

16 Old age

I find that old age has many compensations, and I still feel, as I felt in my youth, that the old should make way for the young and give them their opportunity while they yet have vision to inspire them, energy to perform and time to achieve.

I have never felt that the contemplation of the past, with the knowledge that it cannot come again, need not be a source of sorrow. The emotion is like that aroused by looking through an album of old photographs which recall happy days, and if we find among them the faces of friends who are no more, we are glad to be reminded of the affection we felt for them. Life has been good to me and I am grateful. My delight in it is as keen as ever and I will thankfully accept as many more years as may be granted. But I am fond of change and have welcomed it even when uncertain whether it would be for the better; so although I am very glad to be where I am, I shall not be too distressed when the summons comes to go away. Autumn has always been my favourite season, and evening has been for me the pleasantest time of day. I love the sunlight but I cannot fear the coming of the dark.

Duff Cooper

17 Old age

To me, old age is always fifteen years older than I am.

Bernard Mannes Baruch (1870 - 1965)

18 Old age

To be old, is to be the same but different.
It is frightening, God, but peaceful.
Death is closer, and so are You.
What is done, is done, and cannot be undone.
Life lives on, day by day,
but most of it is over.

How to make these last days count, God?
To live them with courage, with little complaint.
To give and receive small joys.
To teach the best already learned
and to learn yet a little more.

Plain Prayers for a Complicated World (Collins)

 ## Old age

The evening of a well spent life brings its lamps with it.

Joseph Joubert (1754 - 1824)

20 ## Opportunities

A wise man will make more opportunities than he finds.

Francis Bacon (1561 - 1626)

21 ## Opportunities

Seek the first possible opportunity to act on every good resolution you make.

William James (1842 - 1910)

22 ## Opportunities

His was the sort of career that made the Recording Angel think seriously about taking up shorthand.

Nicholas Bentley

23 Opportunities

Next to knowing when to seize an opportunity, the most important thing in life is to know when to forego an advantage.

Benjamin Disraeli (1804 - 1881)

24 Opportunities

When fate throws a knife at you, you can catch it by the blade and severely wound yourself, or you can catch it by the handle and use it to carve a new future for yourself.

25 Optimism

The optimist proclaims that we live in the best of all possible worlds; and the pessimist fears this is true.

James Branch Cabell (1879 - 1958)

26 Originality

As soon as you can say what you think, and not what some other person has thought for you, you are on your way to being a remarkable man.

Sir James Barrie (1860 - 1937)

27 Others

Bread for myself is a material matter;
bread for other people is a spiritual matter.

Nikolai Berdyaev (1874 - 1948)

105

28 Others

In order to imitate Jesus we should realise that we make sense as Christians if we live "for" others, if we see our existence as being a service to our brothers, and make this the foundation of our whole life.

Chiara Lubich

 29 Parents

He who takes the child by the hand takes mother by the heart.

Danish proverb

30 Parents

What a father says to his children is not heard by the world, but it will be heard by posterity.

Jean Paul Eixhter

31 Parents

There are times when parenthood seems nothing but feeding the mouth that bites you.

Peter de Vries

SEPTEMBER

1 | Peace

We could have peace to our heart's content, if only we would not concern ourselves with the things other people are saying and doing, things which are no business of ours. How can a man expect to have lasting peace when he is always minding other people's business, always looking out for the chance of engaging in external activities, so that recollection is only possible in a small degree, or at rare intervals? Blessed are the simple, they shall have peace to their heart's content.

Thomas à Kempis (c.1380 - 1471)

2 | Peace

Peace is possible if it is truly willed; and if peace is possible, it is a duty.

Pope Paul VI (1897 - 1978)

3 | Peace

Peace is born of silence, because silence is the threshold where the soul meets God.

Robin Bruce Lockhart

4 | Peace

If there be righteousness in the heart,
There will be beauty in the character.

107

If there is beauty in the character,
There will be harmony in the home.
If there is harmony in the home,
There will be order in the nation.
When there is order in each nation
There will be peace in the world.

Very old Chinese proverb

5 Peace

Peace of heart – without it no good can make us happy; with it, every trial, even the approach of death, can be borne.

Frederic Ozanam (1813 - 1853)

6 Pentecost

Without the Holy Spirit:
God is far away,
Christ stays in the past,
the Gospel is a dead letter,
the Church is simply an organisation,
authority is a matter of domination,
mission a matter of propaganda,
the liturgy no more than an evocation,
Christian living a slave morality.

But in the Holy Spirit:
the risen Christ is there,
the Gospel is the power of life,
the Church shows forth the life of the Trinity,

authority is a liberating service,
mission is a Pentecost,
the liturgy is both memorial and anticipation,
human action is deified.

Patriarch Athenagoras

7 People

The world is divided into people who do things and people who get the credit. Try, if you can, to belong to the first class. There's far less competition.

Dwight Morrow, in a letter to his son

8 People

A gossip is one who talks to you about others, a bore is one who talks to you about himself, and a brilliant conversationalist is one who talks to you about yourself.

9 Perfection

Do all the good you can,
In all the ways you can,
In all the places you can,
At all the times you can,
To all the people you can,
As long as ever you can.

John Wesley (1703 - 1791)

109

10 Perfection

You will never be sorry
For doing your level best,
For your faith in humanity,
For being kind to the poor,
For asking pardon when in error,
For being generous with an enemy,
For sympathising with the oppressed.

Anon.

11 Perseverance

Nevertheless, whatever the particular objective may be, it is far better to start with the knowledge that we are human and as a consequence limited in what we can do, and that at the end of the day, for all our efforts, the results may not be very spectacular. I know of no substitute in any field of human endeavour for hard work, for clear and realistic thinking and planning, and, most important of all, for perseverance. The person who ferrets away, who never lets go, who, when faced with an impasse or just cannot see what he should do next, is content to wait and relax until something happens to give him an opening, is the one who will usually achieve the most. Without in any way renouncing the need to set our sights high, to be satisfied with nothing less than the best, and to commit ourselves totally and unreservedly to participating in the struggle to build a more liveable world, I have come to believe that the important thing is to keep going and to appreciate that even one small improvement is infinitely worth making. It is the multiplication of many people, each working in their own chosen field and in their own individual way, that brings about genuine change.

Leonard Cheshire

12 Persuasion

It is said that Mr Gladstone could persuade most people of most things, and himself of anything.

Dean W.R. Inge (1860 - 1954)

13 Potential

Poverty was the universal way of life in the coal-mining areas of South Wales during my boyhood there. Nonetheless our community culture was rich. It was rooted in our Christian faith and therefore was uninfluenced by the scale of our possessions.

As I grew in understanding I learned to look at people in terms of their potential when God's Holy Spirit was their inspiration. There is no limit to what God can do when commitment to Him is total. Changed lives are unfailing witnesses to that truth in every generation. It will be so in tomorrow's world, for the two great permanents of history are the unchanging needs of people and the unchanging power and love of God.

Lord Tonypandy (who as George Thomas was Speaker of the House of Commons from 1976 to 1983)

14 Poverty

The rich must live more simply that the poor may simply live.

Dr Charles Birch

15 Poverty

It is very difficult for us humans to accept our basic condition of poverty and yet it presses upon us from all sides. We cannot control our world, we are at the mercy of others and of what often seems to be blind fate. Even our own selves escape us. We are not what we would like to be: inadequacies of all kinds dog us. We are prey to physical and psychological ills. We long to be masters of our lives, in control, strong and beautiful. In a word, gods. The Gospel message is good news to the poor. "Be man, not God." This poverty, revolting as it is to our nature, is blessed when accepted, because it opens us to God, makes us realise our need of a saviour. Aware that we can never find fulfilment in ourselves we are drawn to look to him alone.

Ruth Burrows

16 Poverty

I used to think I was poor. Then they told me I wasn't poor. I was needy. Then they told me it was self-defeating to think of myself as needy; I was deprived. Then they told me deprived was a bad image; I was underprivileged. Then they told me underprivileged was overused; I was disadvantaged. I still don't have a dime. But I sure have a great vocabulary.

Jules Feiffer

17 Poverty

God loves the poor, and consequently He loves those who have an affection for the poor. For when we love anyone very much we also love His friends and servants.

St Vincent de Paul (1581 - 1660)

18 Poverty

It is easy enough to tell the poor to accept their poverty as God's will when you yourself have warm clothes and plenty of food and medical care and a roof over your head and no worry about the rent. But if you want them to believe you – try to share some of their poverty and see if you can accept it as God's will yourself.

Thomas Merton (1915 - 1968)

19 Prayer

He who has learned how to pray has learned the greatest secret of a holy and happy life.

William Law (1686 - 1761)

20 Prayer

I got up early one morning and rushed right into the day. I had so much to accomplish that I didn't have time

113

to pray. Problems just tumbled about me. And heavier became each task. Why did God not help me, I wondered. He answered, "You did not ask." I wanted to see joy and beauty but the day toiled on grey and bleak. I wondered why God did not show me and He said, "You did not seek." I woke up early this morning and paused before entering the day. I had so much to accomplish that I had to take time to pray...

21 Prayer

Lord, I shall be verie busie this day. I may forget Thee but doe not Thou forget me.

Sir Jacob Astley (1579 - 1652)
Prayer before the Battle of Newbury

22 Prayer

Pray as you can, and do not try to pray as you can't. Take yourself as you find yourself, and start from that.

Dom John Chapman, O.S.B. (1865 - 1933)

23 Prayer

If you never had any distractions you do not know how to pray. For the secret of prayer is a hunger for God and for the vision of God, a hunger that lies far deeper than the level of language or affection. And a man whose memory and imagination are persecuting him with a crowd of useless or even evil thoughts and images, may sometimes be forced to pray far better in the depths of his murdered heart than one whose mind is swimming with clear concepts and brilliant purposes and easy acts of love. It is the will to pray that is the essence of prayer, and the desire to find God; to see him and to love him is the one thing that matters.

Thomas Merton (1915 - 1968)

24 Prayer

You pray in your distress
and in your need;
would that you might pray also
in the fullness of your joy and
in your days of abundance.

Kahlil Gibran (1883 - 1931)

25 Prayer

Make your prayer simple, as simple as you can. Reason little, love much, and you will pray well.

Fr Willie Doyle, S.J.

26 Prayer

The self-sufficient do not pray, the self-satisfied will not pray, the self-righteous cannot pray. No man is greater than his prayer life.

Leonard Ravenhill

27 Prayer

Ten Golden Rules

1. Plan to pray; do no leave it to chance. Select a time and a place (a room at home, on the bus, taking a walk).

2. Decide on how long you will spend in trying to pray (five minutes, ten, fifteen, thirty or more).

3. Decide what you are going to do when you pray – e.g., which prayer to select to say slowly and lovingly; or which passage from the Bible to read prayerfully. Sometimes use your own words; sometimes just be still and silent. Follow your inclination.

4. Always start by asking the Holy Spirit for help in your prayers. Pray: "Come Holy Spirit, teach me to pray; help me to do it."

5. Remember you are trying to get in touch with a Person, and that Person is God – Father or Son or Holy Spirit. He is wanting to get in touch with you.

6. Don't be a slave to one way of praying. Choose the one that you find easiest, and try some other method when the one you are using becomes a burden or doesn't help.

7. Don't look for results.

8. If you have distractions, then turn your distractions into your prayer. (If a car passes the window in the wrong gear, then say something to God about the

driver – I mean a kind of prayer for the welfare of the driver, not necessarily for his driving or the gear box!)

9. If you always feel dry and uninterested at prayer, then read a spiritual book or pamphlet. An article in a Catholic paper may be a help. Spiritual reading is important.

10. Trying to pray is praying. Never give up trying.

Cardinal Basil Hume , O.S.B.

28 Prayer

Talk to him in prayer of all your wants, your troubles, even of the weariness you feel in serving him. You cannot speak too freely, too trustfully, to him.

François Fénelon (1651 - 1715)

29 Prayer

One thing is certain: as long as you only pray to God for yourselves, your prayers will not be as perfect as He wishes them to be.

Jean Nicolas Grou (1731 - 1803)

30 Prayer

When I pray, coincidences happen, when I don't, they don't.

Archbishop William Temple (1881 - 1944)

OCTOBER

1 Prayer

I have lived to thank God that all my prayers have not been answered.

Jean Ingelow (1820 - 1897)

2 Prayer

After I enter the chapel I place myself in the presence of God and I say to him. "Lord, here I am; give me whatever you wish." If he gives me something, then I am happy and I thank him. If he does not give me anything, then I thank him nonetheless, knowing, as I do, that I deserve nothing. Then I begin to tell him of all that concerns me, my joys, my thoughts, my distress, and finally, I listen to him.

St Catherine Labouré (1806 - 1870)

3 Prayer

If Christ himself needed to retire from time to time to the mountain top to pray, lesser men need not be ashamed to acknowledge that necessity.

B.H. Streeter

4 Prayer

The Godward movement means putting yourself near God, with God, in a time of quietness every day. You put yourself with him just as you are, in the feebleness of your concentration, in your lack of warmth and desire, not trying to manufacture pious thoughts or phrases. You put yourself with God, empty perhaps, but hungry and thirsty for him; and if in sincerity you cannot say that you want God you can perhaps tell him that you want to want him; and if you cannot say even that perhaps you can say that you want to want to want him! Thus you can be very near him in your naked sincerity. You are "with God" not by achieving certain devotional exercises in his presence but by daring to be your own self as you reach towards him.

Lord Ramsey of Canterbury (1904 - 1988)

5 Prayer

Two prisoners pray

I went back to my cell
The night before my hearing;
I decided to make a prayer.
I had to be on my knees...
I couldn't play it cheap.
So I waited until the thin kid was asleep,
then I quietly climbed down from my bunk
and bent my knees...

I knelt at the foot of the bed
and told God what was in my heart.
I made like He was there in the flesh with me.
I talked to Him plain...
no big words, no almighties...
I talked to Him like I had wanted to talk

to my old man so many years ago.
I talked like a little kid and I told Him of
my wants and lacks, of my hopes and disappointments.
I asked the Big Man...
I felt like I was someone
that belonged to somebody who cared.
I felt like I could even cry if I wanted to,
something I hadn't been able to do for years.
"God," I concluded, "maybe I won't be an angel
but I do know I'll try not to be a blank.
So in your name, and in Cisto's name, I ask this. Amen."

A small voice added another amen to mine
I looked up and saw the thin kid, his elbows bent,
his head resting on his hand.
I peeped through the semidarkness to see his face,
wondering if he was sounding me.
But his face was like mine, looking for help from God.
There we were, he lying down,
head on bended elbow, and I still on my knees.
No one spoke for a long while.
Then the kid whispered,
"I believe in God also.
Maybe you don't believe it, but I used to go to church,
and I had the hand of God on me.
I felt always like you and I feel now,
warm, quiet, and peaceful,
like there's no suffering in our hearts."

"What's it called, Chico, this what we feel?"
I asked softly.
"It's Grace by the Power of the Holy Spirit."

The kid said.
I didn't ask any more.
There in the semidarkness
I had found a new sense of awareness.

6 Prayer

These things, good Lord, that we pray for, give us Thy grace to labour for.

St Thomas More (1478 - 1535)

7 Preaching

If teaching and preaching is your job, then study diligently and apply yourself to whatever is necessary for doing the job well. Be sure that you first preach by the way you live. If you do not, people will notice that you say one thing, but live otherwise, and your words will bring only cynical laughter and a derisive shake of the head.

St Charles Borromeo (1538 - 1584)

8 Preaching

I'd rather see a sermon
Than hear one any day.
I'd rather one would walk with me
Than merely show the way.
The eye's a better pupil
And more willing than the ear;

Fine counsel is confusing
But example is always clear.
For I may misunderstand you
And the high advice you give;
But there's no misunderstanding
How you act and live.

Edgar Albert Guest (1881 - 1959)

9 Preaching

What you do speaks so loud that I cannot hear what you say.

Ralph Waldo Emerson (1803 - 1883)

10 Preaching

Few sinners are saved after the first twenty minutes of a sermon.

Mark Twain (1835 - 1910)

11 Presence of God

God often visits us – but most of the time we are not at home.

French proverb

12 Priesthood

Beware of spending too much time doing the work of the Lord without spending enough time with the Lord of the work!

Pope John Paul II to priests

13 Priesthood

The priesthood is a passionate commitment, a fiery-eyed vision, and an insatiable thirst for holiness and practical justice. The priest is called to be challenger, enabler, life-giver, poet of life, music maker, dreamer of dreams. He must be a man of personal faith, conformed to Christ, a man who loves the scriptures, draws sustenance from the sacramental life of the Church, and truly knows the community with and for whom he offers sacrifice. A priest is a man with a clear sense of his own self, and one who strives to develop all his natural talents to the limit for the good of the Church. He is a man of unreasonable hopes and expectations, who takes seriously, for himself and others, the injunction to be perfect as the heavenly Father is.

Cardinal Joseph Bernardin

14 Priesthood

Chaucer's Parson

A holy-minded man of good renown
There was, and poor, the parson to a town,
Yet he was rich in holy thought and work...

He found sufficiency in little things.
Wide was his parish with houses far asunder
Yet he neglected not in rain or thunder,
In sickness or in grief, to pay a call
On the remotest, whether great or small,
Upon his feet, and in his hand a stave.

This noble example to his sheep he gave,
First following the word before he taught it
And it was from the gospel he had caught it...
His business was to show a fair behaviour
And draw men thus to Heaven and their Saviour.

Geoffrey Chaucer (1340? - 1400)

15 Progress

The world is moving so fast these days that the man who says it can't be done is generally interrupted by someone doing it.

Elbert Hubbard (1856 - 1915)

16 Reasons

We are generally the better persuaded by the reasons we discover than by those given to us by others.

Blaise Pascal (1623 - 1662)

17 Reasons

There's a reason

For every pain that we must bear,
For every burden, every care,
There's a reason.
For every grief that bows the head,
For every teardrop that is shed,
There's a reason.

125

For every hurt, for every plight,
For every lonely, pain-racked night,
There's a reason.
But if we trust God as we should,
It all will work out for our good,
He knows the reason.

18 Remembrance

The Few

Mischievous laughing boys grew,
  To quick manhood to be "The Few"
Who flew beyond all human call,
  Through summer height to autumn fall.
Infringed the sanctity of space,
  In freedom's name – and died in grace,
Falling like leaves upon the weald,
  To russet spot on field.
Their brief, gay, valiant season spent,
  For us. Our task, their monument.
Nature herself has taken o'er,
  And has decreed for evermore,
The Few shall be remembered
  If not by you. Well then by me.

This poem was written by an 18-year-old Pilot Air Gunner
from Tipperary, the day before he was killed in Arnhem,
and was found in his tunic

19 | Repentance

You cannot repent too soon, because you do not know how soon it may be too late.

Thomas Fuller (1608 - 1661)

20 | Respect

Our first task in approaching
    another people
      another culture
        another religion
is to take off our shoes
for the place we are approaching is holy.
Else we may find ourselves
treading on another man's dream.
More serious still we may forget...
that God was there before our arrival.

Anon.

21 | Respect

Eternal Father, source of life and light,
whose love extends to all people,
all creatures, all things:
grant us that reverence for life
which becomes those who believe in you,
lest we despise it, degrade it,
or come callously to destroy it.
Rather let us save it, secure it,

and sanctify it, after the example
of your Son, Jesus Christ our Lord.

Archbishop Robert Runcie

 ## Resurrection

The gospels do not explain the resurrection; the resurrection explains the gospels. Belief in the resurrection is not an appendage to the Christian faith; it is the Christian faith.

J.S. Whale

 ## Resurrection

Every parting gives a foretaste of death,
every reunion a hint of the resurrection.

Arthur Schopenhauer (1788 - 1860)

 ## Right and Wrong

A long habit of not thinking a thing wrong gives it a superficial appearance of being right.

Thomas Paine (1737 - 1809)

Sabbath

In the tempestuous ocean of time and toil there are islands of stillness where man may enter a harbour and reclaim his dignity. The island is the seventh day, the Sabbath, a day of detachment from things, instruments, and practical affairs, as well as of attachment to the spirit.

Abraham Heschel

26 Scriptures

Just as at the sea those who are carried away from the direction of the habour bring themselves back on course by a clear sign, on seeing a tall beacon light or some mountain peak coming into view, so Scripture may guide those adrift on the sea of life back into the harbour of the divine will.

St Gregory of Nyssa (c.330 - 395)

27 Service

The question which divides men nowadays is no longer politics: it is a social question. It is whether to choose the spirit of egotism or the spirit of service.

It is whether society is a great exploitation to profit the strong, or a consecration of every man for the good of all, and above all, for the protection of the weak.

Frederic Ozanam (1813 - 1853)

28 Service

We will find that it is in going out to help someone whose need is greater than ours that we solve our own problems and become fulfilled as a person, more fully the unique masterpiece, that God wills us ultimately to be.

Leonard Cheshire

129

29 Sick, the

You are the aristocracy of the kingdom of God... and if you but choose to do so, you work out with Him the world's salvation. This is the Christian understanding of suffering; it is the only one that puts your heart at rest.

Pope Paul VI (1897 - 1978)
speaking to the sick and suffering people
of the world at the end of the Second Vatican Council

30 Silence

Behold, my beloved, I have shown you the power of silence, how thoroughly it heals and how fully pleasing it is to God... know that it is by silence that the saints grow, that it was because of silence that the power of God dwelt in them and because of silence that the mysteries of God were known to them.

Ammonas, a disciple of St Antony (c.350)

31 Silence

The more we receive in silent prayer, the more we can give in active life. We need silence in order to be able to touch souls. The essential thing is not what we say, but what God says to us and through us. All our words will be useless unless they come from within. Words which do not give the light of Christ increase the darkness.

Mother Teresa of Calcutta

NOVEMBER

1 | Simplicity

The older I grow the more clearly I perceive the dignity
and winning beauty of simplicity in thought, conduct
and speech; a desire to simplify all that is complicated
and to treat everything with the greatest naturalness
and clarity. I must strip my vines of all useless foliage
and concentrate on what is truth, justice and charity.

Pope John XXIII (1881 - 1963)

2 | Simplicity

All the truly deep people have at the core of their being
the genius to be simple or to know how to seek simplicity. The inner and outer aspects of their lives match;
there is something transparent about them. They may
keep the secret of their existence in a private preserve,
but they are so uncluttered by any self-importance
within, so unthreatened from without that they have
what one philosopher called a certain "availability",
they are ready to be at the disposal of others.

Martin Marty

3 | Sin

The greatest of faults, I should say, is to be conscious of
none.

Thomas Carlyle (1795 - 1881)

4 | Sin

Sin has four characteristics:
self-sufficiency instead of faith,
self-will instead of submission,
self-seeking instead of benevolence,
self-righteousness instead of humility.

E. Paul Hovey

5 | Sin

All sin is a form of self-exaltation, the attempt to be the author of one's own happiness rather than to receive this happiness from God. The effort to create this happiness for himself, an utterly impossible accomplishment for man, constitutes sin in its most basic form. Man cannot produce the deepest values in human life; they can only be received. It is God alone who can give ultimate fulfillment, complete peace, and if man tries to achieve these values by himself, he is doomed to fail. This attempt we call sin.

Peter G. van Breemen, S.J.

6 | Sin

He alone has a right to despair whose sins are as great as the mercy of God.

St Augustine of Hippo (354 - 430)

7 Solitude

Only experience reveals what benefits the solitude and silence of the desert bring to those who love it.

St Bruno (c.1032 - 1101)

8 Solitude

Solitude is an ocean with wonderful places hidden in its depths.

Isaac of Nineveh (d. c.680)

9 Solitude

All the troubles of life come upon us because we refuse to sit quietly for a while each day in our rooms.

Blaise Pascal (1623 - 1662)

10 Solitude

The heart must learn to live in its desert if it is to be capable of involvement in the market place. It is only in the desert that we can learn to turn loneliness into solitude, and it is only when we have learned solitude and freedom – the capacity to be alone – that we can be safely involved with others.

Cardinal Basil Hume, O.S.B.

11 Solitude

Solitude is the audience chamber of God.

Walter Savage Landor (1775 - 1864)

12 Suffering

No man ever deserved suffering less, and no man ever experienced suffering more terrible. He had done nothing but love people; he had lived a life of moral and spiritual perfection; and yet he came to the end in the agony of the Cross. There is nothing that we have to experience which Jesus has not already experienced. And it is because he went through it himself that he is able to help others who are going through it too.

William Barclay (1907 - 1978)

13 Suffering

Suffering by itself is nothing; it's useless. But suffering shared with Christ in his passion is a wonderful gift to human life. It is the most beautiful gift for us to share in the passion of Christ, yes, and a sign of love, because His Father proved that He loved the world by giving His Son to die for us, and so in Christ's own life it was proved that suffering was the gift, the greatest gift. As Our Lord has said, "Greater love than this no man has that he gives his life for his friends." And so when we suffer for Jesus, this is the greatest love, the undivided love.

Mother Teresa of Calcutta

14 Suffering

The little ills we have are, I believe, a blessing. Without them we would not know how to appreciate all we've had in the past or we'd never think about a better life to come.

Hilda Burke

15 Suffering

Michael was born a helpless cripple, unable to do anything for himself. His mind was right, but everything else was wrong.

He was never out of a hospital since birth. The hospital was run by nuns and he grew up with them.

> He was a most attractive boy.
> Everyone loved him.

One day a surgeon, new and very clever, thought that, with new techniques discovered in America, he would be able to make this boy walk. He studied these techniques and came back from the U.S.A. sure that he could cure the boy.

> Michael would walk.

You can imagine the tremendous excitement in that hospital. Michael had been the centre of interest for years. Everybody, including the surgeon, went to Mass and received Holy Communion on the morning of the operation.

The day-long operation was successful and the following week they had a Mass of thanksgiving.

> Everyone was full of joy.
> Suddenly their hopes were dashed.
> Clots started forming in the veins.
> The dying boy remained cheerful.

A day or two before Michael died a priest who had known him since childhood, was sitting by his bed saying the Rosary. Tears were running down his cheeks.

When Michael saw this he said: "Father, surely you are not crying!"

The priest replied: "Michael, I am terribly disappointed. Everybody is. We had such great hopes for you."

Michael said: "Father, I can't understand you. I have never been outside this hospital. I have known only love since I was born. But I was going to leave. Since I was born, I have never had a chance of doing wrong. If I had been able to walk, perhaps I would have walked into evil ways. God has spared me and now I am going to him."

There is one answer to the question about "useless people".

Cardinal John Heenan (1905 - 1975)

16 Suffering

To her, every moment was precious even if it brought pain, and existence was significant and meaningful even if she was confined to bed. To her, sufferings were but a means of joining Christ in the redemption of mankind. She lived in love, she reflected love, and she died in love. From her misery she forged triumph. For her, indeed, to live was Christ and to die was to go to the eternal Lover whose presence she had come to know in suffering. The story of her suffering is beautiful. By accepting her calvary she brought peace for herself and for others.

Murray Ballantyne, writing of a young friend of his dying of tuberculosis

17 Suffering

Pain in the hands of God can be a wonderful thing, I found. It is one of God's ways of unclasping the fingers that otherwise might cling too closely to the world.

Rev T.W. Bradburne's last letter to his son John

18 Thanksgiving

Gratitude is born in hearts that take time to count up past mercies.

Charles E. Jefferson (1860 - 1937)

19 Thanksgiving

We should at least spend as much time thanking God for his favours as we have spent in asking them.

St Vincent de Paul (1581 - 1660)

20 Thanksgiving

Would you know who is the greatest saint in the world? It is not he who prays most or fasts most; it is not he who gives most alms, but it is he who is always thankful to God, who receives everything as an instance of God's goodness and has a heart always ready to praise God for it.

If anyone would tell you the shortest, surest way to all happiness and perfection, he must tell you to make a rule to thank and praise God for everything that happens to you. Whatever seeming calamity happens to you, if you thank God and praise God for it, you turn it into a blessing. Could you therefore work miracles you could not do more for yourself than by this thankful spirit; it turns all that it touches into happiness.

William Law (1686 - 1761)

21 Thoughts

A great many people think they are thinking when they are merely rearranging their prejudices.

William James (1842 - 1910)

22 Time

Do not look forward to the changes and chances of this life with fear. Rather, look to them with full confidence, that, as they arise, God to whom you belong will in His love enable you to profit by them.

He has guided and guarded you thus far in life. Do you but hold fast to His dear hand, and He will lead you safely through all trials. Whenever you cannot stand, He will carry you lovingly in His arms.

Do not look forward to what may happen tomorrow. The same Eternal Father who cares for you today will take care of you tomorrow and every day of your life. Either He will shield you from suffering or He will give you unfailing strength to bear it. Be at peace then, and put aside all useless thoughts, all vain dreads and all anxious imaginations.

St Francis de Sales (1567-1622)

23 Time

God, I spend so much time reliving yesterday or antici-
pating tomorrow that I lose sight of the only time which
is really mine – the present... That's all I have – all I ever
will. Give me the faith that knows that each moment
contains exactly what is best for me. Give me the hope
that trusts you enough to forget past sins and future
trials. Give me that love that makes each minute of life
an anticipation of eternity with you.

Anon.

24 Time

If I have a philosophy of life, it is that we only come this
way once, we only get one go at it, and I would hate to
think when my time comes to die that I had not used up
every opportunity and every bit of life that had been
offered.

Angela Rippon

25 Time

God has created me to do him some definite service: He
has committed some work to me which he has not
committed to another. I have my mission – I may never
know it in this life, but I shall be told it in the next.

I am a link in a chain, a bond of connection between
persons. He has not created me for nothing. I shall do
good; I shall do his work.

Therefore I will trust him. Whatever, wherever I am, I cannot be thrown away. If I am in sickness, my sickness may serve him; in perplexity, my perplexity may serve him; if I am in sorrow, my sorrow may serve him. He does nothing in vain. He knows what he is about. He may take away my friends. He may throw me among strangers. He may make me feel desolate, make my spirits sink, hide my future from me – still he knows what he is about.

Cardinal John Henry Newman (1801 - 1890)

26 Time

God give me work till my life shall end
and life till my work is done.

Winifred Holtby, her epitaph

27 Time

No man ever sank under the burden of the day. It is when tomorrow's burden is added to the burden of today that the weight is more than a man can bear. Never load yourself so. If you find yourself loaded so, at least remember this: it is your own doing, not God's. He begs you to leave the future to him, and mind the present.

George Macdonald (1824 - 1905)

28 Trust

My life is but a weaving
    Between my God and me;

I may not choose the colours,
      He knows what they should be;
For He can view the pattern
      From the upper side
While I can see it only
      On this the under side.

Sometimes He weaveth sorrow,
      Which seemeth strange to me:
But I will trust His judgement,
      And work on faithfully;
'Tis He who fills the shuttle,
      He knows what is best;
So I shall weave in earnest
      And leave with Him the rest.

At last when life is ended,
      With Him I shall abide,
Then I may view the pattern
      Upon the upper side;
Then I shall know the reason
      Why pain with joy entwined
Was woven in the fabric
      Of life that God designed.

29   Trust

I will not mistrust him, Meg, though I shall feel myself weakening and on the verge of being overcome with fear. I shall remember how Saint Peter at a blast of wind began to sink because of his lack of faith, and I shall do as he did; call upon Christ and pray to him for help. And then I trust he shall place his holy hand on me and the stormy seas hold me up from drowning.

St Thomas More (1478 - 1535)

30 Trust

Footprints

One night a man had a dream. He dreamed he was walking along the beach with the LORD. Across the sky flashed scenes from his life. For each scene, he noticed two sets of footprints in the sand: one belonging to him, and the other to the LORD.

When the last scene of his life flashed before him, he looked back at the footprints in the sand. He noticed that many times along the path of his life there was only one set of footprints. He also noticed that it happened at the very lowest and saddest times in his life.

This really bothered him and he questioned the LORD about it, "Lord, you said that once I decided to follow you, you'd walk with me all the way. But I have noticed that during the most troublesome times in my life there is only one set of footprints. I don't understand why when I needed you most you would leave me."

The LORD replied, "My precious, precious child, I love you and I would never leave you. During your times of trial and suffering, when you see only one set of footprints, it was then that I carried you."

Amen.

DECEMBER

1 Trust

All shall be well and all shall be well and all manner of things shall be well.

Dame Julian of Norwich (1343 - 1443)

2 Trust

My Lord God, I have no idea where I am going. I do not see the road ahead of me. I cannot know for certain where it will end. Nor do I really know myself, and the fact that I think I am following your will does not mean that I am actually doing so. But I believe that the desire to please you does in fact please you. And I hope I have that desire in all that I am doing. I hope that I will never do anything apart from that desire. And I know that as I do this you will lead me by the right road though I may know nothing about it. Therefore will I trust you always though I may seem to be lost and in the shadow of death. I will not fear, for you are ever with me, and you will never leave me to face my perils alone.

Thomas Merton (1915 - 1968)

3 Trust

The pinnacle of faith is total trust, and anyone who has scaled this pinnacle has found heaven on earth because the fruit of total trust is "the peace that passes all understanding."

Delia Smith

4 Trust

I think the zest for mortification and spiritual effort is something that waxes and wanes... It is a mistake to try to force oneself to feel enthusiasms which are just not there. Put yourself completely in God's hands; he is more concerned for your spiritual welfare than you are – loves you so very much more than you love yourself... Utter trust in God is the deepest thing in life. God's unbounded love lavished on each one of us... as if each of us were the only pearl of great price. To take us, each of us, for his own, Christ "sold all that he had", sold it on the Cross – and rose from the dead to assure us that "all is well".

Bishop Christopher Butler, O.S.B. (1902 - 1986)

5 Truth

Truth is the foundation of all knowledge and the cement of all societies.

John Dryden (1631 - 1700)

6 Truth

Be so true to thyself as thou be not false to others.

Francis Bacon (1561 - 1626)

7 Truth

Neither a borrower nor a lender be;
For loan oft loses both itself and friend,

And borrowing dulls the edge of husbandry.
This above all – to thine own self be true,
And it must follow, as the night the day,
Thou canst not then be false to any man.

William Shakespeare (1564 - 1616)
Polonius in Hamlet

8 | Unemployment

Beatitudes in time of unemployment

Blessed are they who deprive themselves in order to invest and create new jobs, for they will accumulate shares in the Kingdom.

Blessed are they who give up the second jobs, which they do not need in order to live with dignity, for they will be assured of a place in the Kingdom.

Blessed are those public employees who take a personal interest in their duties, who reduce the formalities and who face problems conscientiously, for their work will be regarded as something holy.

Blessed are those in the professions who do not stand in the way of justifiable reforms within these professions, for it is better to be right with God than with one's colleagues.

Blessed are those workers and employees who put creation of new jobs for all before their own overtime pay or rise in salary, for they know where their real riches lie.

147

Blessed are those workers who do not defraud social security by claiming to be unemployed when they are not, for by not doing so they deprive the rich of the justification for their own egoism.

Blessed are those bankers, middle-men and business-men who do not take advantage of the necessity of others in order to increase their own assets, even by legal means, for they will be doing a great service to the cause of peace.

Blessed are those politicians and trade unionists who strive to find realistic solutions to the problem of unemployment, without regard for party policies and interests, for they will hasten the coming of the Kingdom.

Blessed will we all be when we stop saying: "If I do not take advantage of the situation, someone else will"; when we stop thinking, "As long as I do not break the law, I can do what I want," for then life in society will be an anticipation of the happiness of the Kingdom.

Bishop Rafael Torija of Ciudad Real, Spain,
and his Council of Priests

9 Unity

In order to be united we must love one another, to love one another we must know one another, to know one another we must meet one another.

Cardinal Mercier (1851 - 1926)
Testament

10 Unity

The lesson must surely be that true collaboration does not mean merely working alongside one another but genuine sharing. Even where there is a difference in calling and some quite profound differences in belief, there may still be sharing. Christian partners do not have to be identical. Sharing can itself add a dimension to combined activity. The criterion we follow in responding to a call for joint action, or for "the double act" at a meeting or religious service [is]: "Where one plus one can add up to more than two." To achieve that sort of sharing, it often happens that other things may be shared as well. Perhaps the most important of all is shared prayer. Sharing does not always mean possession in common. The sharing of minds is at least as important as the sharing of resources. That will come only through knowledge and trust, which result from habitual sharing.

David Sheppard and Derek Worlock

11 Value

'Twas battered, and scarred, and the auctioneer
Thought it was scarcely worth his while
To waste his time on the old violin.
But held it up with a smile.

"What am I bidden, good people," he cried.
"Who'll start the bidding for me?
A dollar. A dollar. Then two, only two!

DECEMBER

Two dollars, and who'll make it three.
Three dollars once; three dollars twice.
　　　Going for three. –" But, no –
From the room far back a grey-haired man
Came forward and picked up the bow,
Then wiping the dust from the old violin
And tightening the loose strings,
He played a melody pure and sweet
As sweet as an Angel sings.

The music ceased, and the auctioneer,
With a voice that was soft and low,
Said, "What am I bid for the old violin?"
And he held it up with the bow.
"A thousand dollars, who'll make it two?
Two thousand! And who'll make it three?
Three thousand, once, three thousand twice,
And going, and gone," said he.
The people cheered but some of them cried,
"We do not quite understand,
What changed its worth." Swift came the reply,
　　　"The touch of the master's hand."

And many a man with life out of tune,
And battered and torn with sin,
Is auctioned cheap to a thoughtless crowd
　　　Much like the old violin.

A "mess of pottage", a glass of wine,
A game and he travels on.
He's "going" once. He's "going" twice.
He's "going" and almost "gone".
But the Master comes and the foolish crowd

Never can quite understand,
The worth of a soul, and the change that's wrought
By the touch of the Master's hand.

Myra Brooks Welch

12 Value

Do not be known as a man of success; be known as a man of value.

Albert Einstein (1879 - 1955)

13 Value

A man who knows the price of everything and the value of nothing.

Oscar Wilde (1854 - 1900), definition of a cynic

14 Values

Our values are the guides by which we navigate ourselves through life.

Poster

15 Virtues

Most high, glorious God, enlighten the darkness of my heart and give me, Lord, a correct faith, a certain hope, a perfect charity, sense, and knowledge, so that I may carry out your holy and true command.

St Francis of Assisi (1181 - 1226)

16 Vocation

Our Lord has created persons for all states in life, and in all of them we see people who have achieved sanctity by fulfilling their obligations well.

St Anthony Mary Claret (1807 - 1870)

17 Vocation

When I have learned to do the Father's will,
I shall have fully realized my vocation.

Carlo Carretto

18 Wisdom

O gracious and holy Father, give us wisdom to perceive thee, diligence to seek thee, patience to wait for thee, eyes to behold thee, a heart to meditate upon thee, and a life to proclaim thee; through the power of the Spirit of Jesus Christ our Lord.

St Benedict of Nursia (480 - 543)

19 Wisdom

It is an ironic fact that in this nuclear age
when the horizon of human knowledge
and human experience
has passed far beyond any
that any age has ever known,

that we turn back at this time
to the older source of wisdom and strength,
to the words of the prophets and the saints,
who tell us that faith is more powerful than doubt,
that hope is more potent than despair,
and that only through the love
that is sometimes called charity
can we conquer those forces
within ourselves
and throughout all the world
that threaten the very existence of mankind.

John Fitzgerald Kennedy (1917 - 1963)

20 Wisdom

And still they gaz'd, and still the wonder grew,
That one small head could carry all he knew.

Oliver Goldsmith (1730 - 1774)

21 Wonder

Wonder is one of the faculties most easy to lose: we
have it in childhood, undiscriminating no doubt but
vivid and deep; we all too easily lose it as we grow older
and become immersed in our daily concerns; and so,
unless we are very careful, not beauty only but life itself
passes us by. For inevitably life loses its meaning when
it loses its mystery.

Gerald Vann, O.P. (1906 - 1963)

153

DECEMBER

 ## Wonder

22

We die on the day when our lives cease to be illumined by the steady radiance renewed daily, of a wonder, the source of which is beyond reason.

Dag Hammarskjöld (1905 - 1961)

 ## Words

23

Words of comfort skillfully administered are the oldest therapy known to man.

George Bernard Shaw (1856 - 1950)

Work

24

It is not only prayer that gives glory to God but work,
      smiting on an anvil, sowing a beam,
      white-washing a wall, driving horses,
      reaping, scouring, everything gives God glory.
It being in his grace, you do it as your duty.
To go to Communion worthily gives God great glory,
      but simply to take food in thankfulness
      and temperance gives God glory too.
To lift up the hands in prayer gives God glory.
      But a man with a dung-fork in his hand
      or a woman with a slop-pail,
They give God glory too.
All things give God glory if you mean they should.
So then, my brethren, this is the way to live.

Gerard Manley Hopkins, S.J. (1844 - 1889)

154

25 December 25th

The darkest time in the year,
The poorest place in the town,
    Cold, and in a taste of fear,
Man and woman alone,
    What can we hope for here?
More light than we can learn,
    More wealth than we can treasure,
More love than we can earn,
    More peace than we can measure,
Because one child is born.

Christopher Fry

26 Work

Work is the natural exercise and function of man...
Work is not primarily a thing one does to live, but the
thing one lives to do. It is, or should be, the full expression of the worker's faculties, the thing in which he
finds spiritual, mental and bodily satisfaction, and the
medium in which he offers himself to God.

Dorothy L. Sayers (1893 - 1957)

27 Work

If I use my faculties and my resources to their full
potential, limited and faulty though these may be, I feel
that I can expect that the Providence of God will make
good whatever I cannot do myself, provided, of course,
that what I am doing is in conformity with His will. Yet

I emphasize the absolute necessity of working as if everything depended upon yourself, for I hold no brief for the view that if only you have sufficient faith you can sit back and God will provide.

Leonard Cheshire

28 Youth

When we are out of sympathy with the young, then I think our work in this world is over.

George Macdonald (1824 - 1905)

29 Youth

Youth is not a time of life; it is a state of mind... It is the freshness of the deep springs of life.

Nobody grows old merely by living a number of years. People grow old by deserting their ideals... Whether sixty or sixteen, every human being may experience wonder,... the undaunted challenge of events, the unfailing childlike appetite for the future, the joy in living. For you are as young as your faith, as old as your doubt; as young as your self-confidence, as old as your despair.

As long as your heart receives messages of beauty, hope, cheer, courage and power from God and from your fellow men, you are young.

30 Youth

To the young I enjoy talking about our work with special pleasure and with the most intense hope. It is a paradox of our time that we have "a generation of concern" growing up in a world dominated at almost every level of society by the disease of materialism and greed. Hence, I am convinced we have a right and obligation to make sure that the concerned, including the youngest of them, know exactly what our problems are among the neglected, impoverished, sick and handicapped, and how concern for them can be expressed in positive action. Too often hospitals, for instance, are unfamiliar areas and the people living there unreal, so that the artificial divisions between the sick and those leading "normal lives" persist in quite an unnecessary way.

Sue Ryder

31 December 31

Let us bid farewell to the past year. It was a year of the Lord, a year of his grace, even a year of growth in the interior life, even if we did not perceive this, because it is in our weakness that God's strength must triumph. And so at the end of the year we can all truly praise God and thank and glorify him for he is good and his mercy endures.

Karl Rahner, S.J. (1904 - 1984)

Names

à Kempis, Thomas: *Peace*
Allen, Fred: *Conferences*
Allyn, Stanley C.: *Humanity*
Alexander, Archibald: *Jesus Christ*
Amiel, Henri Frederic: *Education, Individuality*
Ammonas: *Silence*
Andrew, Fr: *Love*
Anthony Mary Claret, St: *Vocation*
Aristotle: *Goodness*
Astley, Sir Jacob: *Prayer*
Athanasius of Alexandria, St: *Incarnation*
Athenagoras, Patriarch: *Pentecost*
Augustine, St: *God, Martyrdom, Mercy, Sin*
Aurobindo: *Loneliness*

Bacon, Francis: *Opportunities, Truth*
Balfour, Arthur James: *Attitudes*
Ballantyne, Murray: *Suffering*
Barclay, William: *Goodness, Suffering*
Barrie, Sir James M.: *Happiness, Originality*
Baruch, Bernard: *Old age*
Baxter, Richard: *Death*
Bea, Cardinal Augustin: *Forgiveness, Human relationships*
Beecher, Henry Ward: *Christian, Forgiveness*
Bell, Ralph S.: *God*

Belloc, Hillaire: *Friendship*
Benedict, St: *Wisdom*
Benson, Robert Hugh: *Friendship*
Bentley, Nicholas: *Opportunities*
Berdyaev, Nikolai: *Others*
Bernardin, Cardinal Joseph: *Priesthood*
Birch, Charles: *Poverty*
Bonhoeffer, Dietrich: *Jesus Christ*
Boylan, Eugene: *Love*
Bradburne, T.W.: *Suffering*
Brooks Welch, Myra: *Value*
Bruno, St: *Solitude*
Burke, Edmund: *Evil*
Burke, Hilda: *Suffering*
Burrows, Ruth: *Poverty*
Butler, Bishop Christopher: *Trust*

Cabell, James Branch: *Optimism*
Carlyle, Thomas: *Sin*
Catherine Labouré, St: *Prayer*
Challoner, Richard: *Holiness*
Chapman, Dom John: *Prayer*
Charles Borromeo, St: *Preaching*
Chaucer, Geoffrey: *Priesthood*
Cheshire, Leonard: *Perseverance, Service, Work*
Chesterton, G.K.: *Church, Mercy*
Christensen, James L.: *Christian*
Chrysostom, St John: *God*
Churchill, Sir Winston: *Fanaticism*
Clare, Brother: *Education*

Cleveland, M.C.: *Importance*
Collins, J. Churton: *Adversity*
Confucius: *Humanity*
Cooper, Duff : *Old age*
Carretto, Carlo: *Vocation*
Craik, Dinah: *Friendship*

Davis, P.: *The Handicapped*
Dean, Len: *Death*
Delp, Alfred: *Humanity*
de Foucauld, Charles: *Abandonment, Conversion*
de la Rochefoucauld, François: *Contentment, Humanity*
de Tourville, Abbé: *Love*
de Vries, Peter: *Parents*
Disraeli, Benjamin: *Opportunities*
Donne, John: *Humanity*
Doyle, Eric: *Love*
Doyle, Willie: *Prayer*
Dryden, John: *Truth*

Edmund of Abingdon, St: *Intercession*
Edwards, Tryon: *Conversion*
Einstein, Albert: *Value*
Eixhter, Jean Paul: *Parents*
Emerson, Ralph Waldo: *Encouragement, Merit, Preaching*

Farmer, Leslie: *Calvary*
Feiffer, Jules: *Poverty*
Fénelon, Francois: *Grace of the present moment, Prayer*
Foy, T.: *Communion*

Francis of Assisi, St: *Jesus Christ, Virtues*
Francis de Sales, St: *Friendship, Love, Time*
Frank, Ann: *Good News*
French, Charles W.: *Jesus Christ*
Fry, Christopher: *December 25th*
Fuller, Thomas: *Repentance*

Gabriel Possenti, St: *Mary*
Gandhi, Mahatma: *Christian, Freedom*
Gibran, Kahlil: *Prayer*
Girard, E.F.: *Leadership*
Glassgow, Arnold H.: *Leadership*
Goethe, J.W. von: *Humanity*
Goldsmith, Oliver: *Wisdom*
Gregory of Nyssa, St: *Scriptures*
Grou, Jean Nicolas: *Prayer*
Guest, Edgar Albert: *Preaching*

Hailsham, Lord: *Jesus Christ*
Hale, Edward Everest: *Individuality*
Hammarskjöld, Dag: *Holiness, Wonder*
Haskins, M.L.: *January 1st*
Harries, Bishop Richard: *God*
Heenan, Cardinal John: *Suffering*
Herbert, George: *Mercy, Neighbours*
Hermes, John: *Death*
Herrmann, Nina: *God*
Heschel, Abraham: *Sabbath*

Hoch, Edward Wallis: *Humanity*
Hollings, Michael: *Listening*
Holmes, Oliver Wendell: *Knowledge*
Holtby, Winifred: *Time*
Hopkins, Gerard Manley: *Work*
Houselander, Caryll: *Jesus Christ*
Hovey, E. Paul: *Sin*
Hubbard, Elbert: *Friendship, Progress*
Hughes, John Jay: *Faith*
Hume, Cardinal Basil: *Holiness, Prayer, Solitude*
Hugh, of St Victor: *Learning*
Huxley, Aldous: *Change*
Huxley, T.H.: *Education*

Idle, Christopher: *Mothers*
Ignatius of Antioch, St: *Mary*
Inge, Dean W.R.: *Persuasion*
Ingelow, Jean: *Prayer*
Ingersoll, Robert: *Fathers*
Irenaeus, St: *Humanity, Life*
Isaac of Nineveh: *Solitude*

James, William: *Opportunities, Thoughts*
Jarrett, Bede: *Death*
Jefferson, Charles E.: *Thanksgiving*
John XXIII, Pope: *Simplicity*
John of the Cross, St.: *Christian*
John Paul I, Pope: *Commitment*
John Paul II, Pope: *Mary, Priesthood*

John Vianney, St: *Love*
Johnson, Samuel: *Flattery*
Joubert, Joseph: *Old age*
Julian of Norwich, Dame: *Giving, Trust*
Julie Billiart, St: *God*

Kagawa of Japan: *Jesus Christ*
Kennedy, John F.: *Wisdom*
Kierkegaard, Sören: *Martyrdom, Jesus Christ*
King, Martin Luther: *Concern, God, Injustice*
Kingsley, Charles: *Freedom*
Kipling, Rudyard: *Challenge*
Kirk, Kenneth E.: *Christian*
Kirk, Lisa: *People*
Klein, Calvin: *Decisions*

Landor, Walter Savage: *Solitude*
Larson, Bruce: *Importance*
Law, William: *Happiness, Prayer, Thanksgiving*
Leopold, Prince of Loewenstein: *Experience*
Lewis, C.S.: *Immortality*
Lockhart, Robin Bruce: *Peace*
Lubich, Chiara: *Others*

Macdonald, George: *Time, Youth*
McDonald, Robert David: *Indifference*
McIver, Charles: *Education*
Malaval, François: *Contemplation*
Marty, Martin: *Simplicity*
Mercier, Cardinal: *Unity*

Temple, Archbishop William: *Prayer*
Teresa of Calcutta, Mother: *Love, Silence, Suffering*
Teresa of Avila, St: *God, Learning*
Thoreau, Henry David: *Individuality*

Thomas Aquinas, St: *Mary*
Tillich, Paul: *Acceptance, Loneliness*
Tillotson, John: *Life*
Tolstoy, Leo: *Jesus Christ*
Tonypandy, Lord: *Potential*
Torija, Bishop Rafael: *Unemployment*
Twain, Mark: *Fathers, Happiness, Preaching*
Tzu, Lao: *Kindness*

Underhill, Evelyn: *Joy*

van Breemen, Peter: *Abandonment, Sin*
Vanier, Jean: *Listening*
Vann, Gerald: *Wonder*
Vianney, John St: *Love*
Vincent de Paul, St: *Poverty, Thanksgiving*
von Hügel, Friedrich: *Love*

Welch, Myra Brooks: *Value*
Wesley, John: *Perfection*
Whale, J.S.: *Resurrection*
White, E.B.: *Democracy*
Wilde, Oscar: *Value*
Winchell, Walter: *Gossip*
Winstone, Harold: *Holy Spirit*
Wood, H.G: *God*
Worlock, Archbishop Derek: *Unity*
Wyszynski, Cardinal Stefan: *Friendship, Humanity*

Titles

Abandonment
Acceptance
Action
Adversity
Alone
Asking
Attitudes

Calvary
Challenge
Change
Children
Christian
Christianity
Church
Commitment
Communion
Compassion
Concern
Conferences
Contemplation
Contentment
Conversion
Courtesy
Creed
Criticism
Cross

Death
Death and Bereavement
Decisions
Democracy

Easter
Education

Encouragement
Equality
Evil
Experience

Faith
Fanaticism
Fathers
Fear
Flattery
Forgiveness
Freedom
Friendship

Generosity
Gift
God
Goodness
Good News
Gossip
Grace

Handicapped
Happiness
Holiness
Holy Spirit
Home
Hope
Humanity
Human relationships
Humility

Immortality
Importance
Incarnation

TITLES

Indifference
Individuality
Injustice
Intercession

Jesus Christ
Joy

Kindness
Knowledge

Leadership
Learning
Life
Listening
Loneliness
Love

Mary
Martyrdom
Maturity
Mercy
Merit
Mothers
Motives

Neighbours
Nothing people

Old age
Opportunities
Optimism
Originality
Others

Parents
Peace
Pentecost
People
Perfection
Perseverance
Persuasion
Potential
Poverty
Prayer
Preaching
Presence of God
Priesthood
Progress

Reasons
Remembrance
Repentance
Respect
Resurrection
Right and wrong

Sabbath
Scriptures
Service
Sick
Silence
Simplicity
Sin
Solitude
Suffering

Thanksgiving
Thoughts

Time
Trust
Truth

Unemployment
Unity

Value
Values

Virtues
Vocation

Wisdom
Wonder
Words
Work

Youth

Index of Selected Themes

Advent and Christmas: January 16, 18; February 8-9; April 25; May 29; June 6-21; October 19; December 25.

Bereavement: February 2, 16, 18-19, 21-25, 27; April 5.

Comforting words: January 31; February 1-2, 16, 18-19, 21-25, 27; March 21-23, 26, 31; April 5, 8, 12-15, 21, 24, 28-29; May 1, 17-18, July 1, 10-11, 15, 19, 23, 25-28; August 6, 8-9, 16, 18-19, 24; September 5, 17; October 23, 26; November 12-14, 28; December 4, 11, 16.

Family: January 12, 19; March 15-16; May 11; August 11, 29-31.

Holy Week and Easter: January 30; February 13; March 2; June 8-9; October 22-23.

Humorous: February 4, 28; March 14; April 20; May 4, 21, 31; August 22, 25; September 12; October 10.

Lent: January 13; February 8-9; March 19-23; August 8-9; November 3-6.

Pentecost: May 8-10; September 6, 13.

Self-directed retreat: January 8, 10, 16, 28; February 5; May 5-7; June 7-21; July 13-15; September 1; October 6, 11, 26,30; November 7-11; December 16-18, 24, 26.

Service and concern for others: February 3; April 6, 8; May 7, 24; June 1, 5, 24; July 10-12, 20, 22; August 27-28; September 9-11, 14, 17-18; October 27-28; December 8-10, 30.

Suffering: January 4, 11, 23; February 13-15; May 1, 10; July 1, 10, 16; August 6, 24; September 3; October 17, 29; November 12-17.

Time and opportunity: March 10; April 27; June 30; July 3-9; October 15; November 22-27; December 27, 29, 31.

Trust in God: January 2-3; April 13, 15, 17; May 1, 27-28; June 6, 10-11, 14, 22; July 19, 25; August 8; September 13, 15; November 20, 22-23, 25, 28-30; December 1-4, 11.

Sources and Acknowledgements

Permission to reproduce copyright material in this book is gratefully acknowledged: Collins Publishers: *Plain Prayers for a Complicated World*; *The Water and the Fire* (Gerald Vann); *The Hidden World* (Group Captain Leonard Cheshire); *The Door Wherein I Went* (Lord Hailsham of St Marylebone); *Mother Teresa: Her People and Her Work*, Desmond Doig (ed.); – Daughters of St Paul, Boston: *It is Christ we Preach* (Cardinal Joseph Bernardin); – Gill & Macmillan Ltd, Dublin: *Be Not Afraid* (Jean Vanier); – Oxford University Press, Inc. for use of the Anthology *The Wisdom of the Saints*, Jill Haak Adels (ed.); – Stainer & Bell Ltd, London: *Word Alive: 'What a horrid thing fear is'* (Sylvia Pedder); – Penguin Books Ltd: *Revelations of the Divine Love* (Julian of Norwich), translation, © Clifton Wolters; *Canterbury Tales* (Chaucer), translation © Nevill Coghill; – Mercier Press, Cork: *This Tremendous Lover* (Eugene Boylan); – The Society of Authors on behalf of the Bernard Shaw Estate for any quotations from his works; – Macmillan: *Concerning Prayer* (B.H. Streeter); – Thames Methuen: *Halfway to Heaven* (Bruce Lockhart); – Burns & Oates Ltd: *Everyday Faith* (Karl Rahner, S.J.); – Hodder & Stoughton Ltd: *Searching for God* (Basil Hume, O.S.B); *Better Together* (David Sheppard and Derek Worlock); – *Through the Year with William Barclay*, Denis Duncan (ed.); – SPCK: *The Christian Priest Today* (Michael Ramsey); – Darton, Longman and Todd Ltd: *Hearts Not Garments* (Michael Hollings); – The Tablet Publishing Co. Ltd: *The Tablet*, October 1982, article by Ruth Burrows; – Epworth Press: *Plain Christianity* (J.B. Phillips); *We Saw the Holy City* (Leslie Farmer); – The Focolare Movement for the quotation from Chiara Lubich; – Denis Duncan: *Through the Year with Cardinal Heenan*; – Delia Smith for permission to quote from her article in the *Catholic Herald*, 15 March 1985; – Rosica Colin Ltd: *Time to Love, Time to Die* (Prince Leopold Loewenstein); – Grafton Books: *Old Men Forget* (Duff Cooper); – Dimension Books Inc.: *Called by Name* (Peter G. van Breemen, S.J.); – National Catholic Reporter, P.O. Box 419281, Kansas City, MO 64141: Tribute to Paul Joseph Hermes, by John Hermes.

"Abandonment", Peter G. van Breemen, S.J., in *Called by Name* (Dimension Books). "Acceptance", Paul Tillich, in *The Shaking of the Foundations*. "Calvary", Leslie Farmer, in *We Saw the Holy City* (Epworth Press). "Christianity 3", Henry Ward Beecher, in *Life Thoughts*, "Courtesy", Wilson Mizner (Bloomsbury Pub. Ltd). "Death 10", John Hermes, in *National Catholic Reporter*. "Death 13", Len Dean, in *Reflections from Reality*. "Democracy", E.B. White, in "The Wild Flag" in the *New Yorker*, July 3, 1943. "Experience", Prince Leopold of Loewenstein, in *A Time to Love... a Time to Die* (W.H. Allen). "Forgiveness", Alexander Pope, in *An Essay on Criticism*. "Friendship 2", Elbert Hubbard, in *The Note Book*. "Friendship 10", Hillaire Belloc, in "*Dedicatory Ode*". "God 8", Richard Harries, in *Prayers of Grief and Glory*. "God 13", Nina Herrmann, in *Go Out in Joy* (Readers Digest, Nov. 1978). "Goodness 2", William Barclay, in *Through the Year with William Barclay*, ed. Tony Castle. "Good news", Ann Frank, in *Diary*. "Happiness 2", William Law, in *A Serious Call to a Devout and Holy Life*. "Holiness", Cardinal Basil Hume, O.S.B., in *Searching for God* (Hodder & Stoughton). "Holy Spirit 2", J.B. Phillips, in *Plain Christianity* (Epworth Press). "Holy Spirit 3", Harold Winstone, in *The Hodder Book of Christian Prayers*, ed. Tony Castle

(Hodder and Stoughton). "Home", in *Methodist Diary*. "Hope", Henri J. Nouwen, in *Intimacy*. "Intercession 2", Edmund of Abingdon, in *The Hodder Book of Christian Prayers*, ed. Tony Castle (Hodder and Stoughton). "Injustice", Martin Luther King, in "Letter from the Birmingham jail", in *Atlantic Monthly*, August 1963. "Jesus Christ 15", Lord Hailsham of St Marylebone, in *The Door Wherein I Went* (Collins). "Listening 1", Jean Vanier, in *Be Not Afraid* (Gill and MacMillan). "Listening 3", Michael Hollings, in *Hearts not Garments* (Darton, Longman and Todd). "Love 1", Mother Teresa of Calcutta, in *Mother Teresa: Her People and Her Work*, ed. Desmond Doig (Collins). "Love 10", Abbé de Tourville, in *Letters of Spiritual Direction*. "Love 12", Eugene Boylan, O.C.S.O., in *This Tremendous Lover* (Mercier Press). "Mary 1", Pope John Paul II, in *Daily Meditations* (St Paul Publications). "Mothers", Christopher Idle, in *Prayers for Today's Church* (CPAS Publications). "Old age 1", Duff Cooper, in *Old Men Forget*. "Optimism", James Branch Cabell, in *The Silver Stallion*. "Peace 1", Thomas à Kempis, in *The Imitation of Christ*. "Peace 3", Robin Bruce Lockhart, in *Halfway to Heaven*. "People 2", Lisa Kirk, in *New York American Journal*, March 9, 1854. "Perseverance", Leonard Cheshire, in *The Hidden World* (Collins). "Poverty 15", Ruth Burrows, in *The Tablet*, October, 1982. "Poverty 16", Jules Feiffer, cartoon in *Village Voice*, 1965. "Poverty 18", Thomas Merton, in *Seeds of Contemplation*. "Prayer 1", William Law, in *Serious Call to a Devout and Holy Life*. "Prayer 4", Dom John Chapman, O.S.B., in *Spiritual Letters*. "Prayer 9", Cardinal Basil Hume, O.S.B., *To be a Pilgrim* (St Paul Publications). "Prayer 16", B.H. Streeter, in *Concerning Prayer*. "Prayer 17", Archbishop Michael Ramsey, in *Christian Priest Today*. "Preaching", Edgar Albert Guest, in *Sermons We See*. "Priesthood 2", Cardinal Joseph Bernardin, in *It is Christ we Preach* (Daughters of St Paul, Boston). "Priesthood 3", Geoffrey Chaucer, in *The Canterbury Tales*, trans. Nevill Coghill (Penguin). "Respect 2", Archbishop Robert Runcie, in *The Hodder Book of Christian Prayers*, ed. Tony Castle (Hodder and Stoughton). "Resurrection 2", Arthur Schopenhauer, in *Studies in Pessimism: Psychological Observations*. "Sabbath", Abraham Heschel, in *I Asked for Wonder*, ed. Samuel H. Dresner (Crossroad Publishing Co.). "Service 2", Leonard Cheshire, in *The Hidden World* (Collins). "Simplicity 1", Pope John XXIII, in *Journal of a Soul*. "Simplicity 2", Martin Marty, in *Readers Digest*, April, 1980. "Sin 3", Peter G. van Breemen, S.J., in *Called by Name* (Dimension Books). "Solitude 5", Walter Savage Landor, in *Imaginary Conversations*. "Suffering 1", William Barclay, *Through the Year with William Barclay*. "Suffering 2", Sylvia Pedder, in *World Alive* (Stainer and Bell). "Suffering 3", Cardinal John Heenan, in *Through the Year with Cardinal Heenan*, ed. Tony Castle. "Suffering 5", Murray Ballantyne, in *All or Nothing*. "Thanksgiving 3", William Law, in *Serious Call to a Devout and Holy Life*. "Trust 4", Dame Julian of Norwich, in *Revelations of Divine Love*. "Trust 6", Delia Smith, in *Catholic Herald*, 15 March 1985. "Trust 7", Bishop Christopher Butler, O.S.B., in *Letters*. "Unity", David Sheppard and Derek Worlock, in *Better Together* (Hodder and Stoughton). "Wonder 1", Gerald Vann, O.P., in *The Water and the Fire*. "Work 3", Leonard Cheshire, in *The Hidden World* (Collins). "December 31", Karl Rahner, in *Everyday Faith*. "Wonder", Dag Hammarskjöld, in *Markings*. "Youth", Sue Ryder, in *And the Morrow is Theirs*.

Every effort has been made to ensure the accuracy of copyright acknowledgements. The compiler and publishers of this book apologize for any inadvertent omissions of copyright and will rectify this in future editions where such omissions or infringements are brought to their attention.